ACCELERATED
LEARNING UNLOCKED

40+ EXPERT TECHNIQUES FOR RAPID SKILL
ACQUISITION AND MEMORY IMPROVEMENT. THE
STEP-BY-STEP GUIDE FOR BEGINNERS TO
QUICKLY CUT YOUR STUDY TIME FOR ANYTHING
NEW IN HALF.

John R. Torrance, Productivity Coach

result of the use of the information contained within this document, including, but not limited to, — errors, omissions, or inaccuracies.

TABLE OF CONTENTS

INTRODUCTION

If you've ever found yourself in a quagmire as you attempt to learn something new, you've come to the right book. Learning something new can seem like a daunting task, especially given the range of sources that exist on the topic. With the wealth of information available today, you have more opportunities than ever to discover nearly anything. You can jump on your computer or pick up a book and learn whatever you want. The human mind has that kind of unlimited potential. There's a catch, however: knowing the right techniques that will help you access those parts of your brain that best work for you rather than against you.

The purpose of this book is to get to the very core of accelerated learning and improved memory basics. This guide will prepare you for a new learning adventure. Each chapter is based on proven principles that will help you learn as quickly and as effectively as you can. It will provide a solid foundation for you as you embark on your learning journey, allowing you to understand the "why" behind the theory so you can achieve greater success. It is a roadmap for practical and immediate action so that you can see real results. Ultimately, this text is a balance. It aims to be a combination of both theory and practice in a way that will ultimately give you the understanding required to achieve the outcomes you're looking for.

These words will help stimulate your thoughts, inspire discussion, and lead you towards positive action. Like with many topics, this book covers core principles, so if you want to go more in depth on any one chapter, know that there is plenty out there that will go into greater depth. This book is intended to go in-depth only in ways that are immediately practical to you as a learner. It is liberating, however, to know that none of us (and certainly no one book) will ever be able to explain or instruct the full potential of learning that we as human beings hold. There are so many creative possibilities for learning and for life; the key is it all starts with that critical first step! The longer you wait to take this first step, the longer it will take you to finally achieve what you've only dreamed of accomplishing.

I hope you commit to reading, and make this commitment to yourself: take it one chapter at a time. Doing so will enable you to get where you've always meant to, but never thought you could. I guarantee you have it in you. With the proper tools, focus, and work ethic, you will get there, and I will show you how. I hope this book gets you started, not only on learning a specific new skill, but also on a fascinating, limitless journey that comes from being a life-long learner.

CHAPTER ONE

DEBUNKING FIVE POPULAR MYTHS ON LEARNING

You've made it this far, in life and in your career. In some ways, you may think you know enough. Maybe you think you already know what will work for you when it comes to learning new skills and retaining information. This is, at least in part, true. You do have methods that work and that have brought you to where you are in life. You have a baseline of learning that has served you well. However, chances are you are here because there is more to know, to learn, and you are interested in finding an even better way of doing it.

Regardless of what you know - or what you think you know - there are also certain falsehoods about teaching and learning that most of us have been exposed to and that we, in some ways, carry with us throughout our lives. In this sense, what you have built over time as your understanding of how you learn may be completely wrong - or at the very least, incomplete.

Research on learning and memory in the recent past has demonstrated how our beliefs and intuitions about how we learn are more often than not absolutely incorrect. Trial and error is apparently less scientifically helpful for more complex forms of learning, however helpful it may have once been for our early ancestors' survival techniques. As human beings, we are notoriously bad at rating (or predicting) our own performance. We tend to think we know more than we actually do! Actual comprehension or understanding, the cornerstones of real learning, are more often replaced by our impression of knowing something based on a feeling of familiarity or ease in how the information is presented to us.

Human beings are born with an amazing capacity to learn, and more often than not we barely tap into our full potential. We have an incredible ability to learn a variety of different topics and to go in great depth in specific domains.

In this first chapter, I will overview five of the most popular myths about learning that threaten to mislead you as you set out on your new learning venture. By better understanding these myths, you will be able to analyze where you may have been misguided in the past, and ways you can correct yourself along your learning path. I'll follow up on each myth with new and improved methods of learning you can replace them with that will actually work.

Myth #1: Learning Styles Are Essential To Learning

You may have heard about learning styles as a method for teaching and learning new things. Many people, educators included, believe that learning styles are set for each learner and can be used as a tool for a person's academic and professional career.

The concept of learning styles has come to encompass a large body of commercial materials and educational resources, in theory as a means

4

of primarily helping teachers in the classroom. There are slight variations to models and schemes, and over seventy of them exist in total. Each one in some way classifies learners into a category and provides teachers with tools to assess students and tailor lessons to feed into each of the designated styles. The influence of this view is far-reaching within the educational field, from kindergarten to graduate school, and there is an industry that thrives on providing tests and workbooks for schools and professional development organizations.

A recent study indicates that more than ninety percent of the broader public believes they would learn better if they were taught in one of the designated learning styles. This is, however, based more on what has been referred to as "essentialist" and an automatic way of thinking versus evidence that it actually produces those desired outcomes. Advocates in favor of it claim learning will be less effective (or even ineffective) if learners do not receive instruction that takes into account their learning style. In some way, they believe learning styles will promote better learning outcomes. In the past several years researchers have seriously questioned the extent to which the learning styles method has practical implications in educational contexts. Overwhelmingly, studies suggest that there is very little validity to applications of learning styles as well as too little empirical evidence of its benefits.

On a basic level, there is no adequate evidence from current research that can justify learning styles as the best way to teach and take in new information. Studies that do have an appropriate methodology for testing it (which is a rarity) have even found using this technique can have negative outcomes. Learning styles, in short, are widely believed in and yet unfortunately not supported by scientific study because they don't yield the results they promise; the learning styles model can actually undermine education and learning new skills.

Think about it this way: if you spend time and money tailoring your learning to one particular method, you are neglecting the other methods of learning that would enrich your knowledge base more holistically. You aren't just a visual learner and nothing more. As with many things, this may be a default you are drawn to in certain scenarios or contexts, but it would be limiting for you and your ability to learn new topics if you were to classify yourself as only a visual learner.

What To Do Instead

Researchers have pointed to more action-based learning strategies that involve a customized approach for tackling new skills and topics. When learning something new, it is best if you identify the optimal approach for each kind of subject matter that is based on that particular subject. For instance, if you're an English teacher who has to make a writing course curriculum, you will want to include a heavy verbal emphasis, whereas the most efficient and effective method of teaching geometry will require materials that relate to visual and spatial techniques for learning. Different people will always learn in different ways; that is perhaps the primary lesson we can learn from the learning styles model. What will be more helpful for you moving forward in your learning is how you apply different learning methods to the different skills you want to learn. If you're learning music, you want to engage your auditory learning style. If you want to learn painting, you'll want to choose your visual learning style tool, and so on. The more dextrous you are as a learner, the more likely you will be to find success.

Think of learning as having a toolbox. You want to have as many tools (learning styles) in your toolbox as possible so you can choose the most appropriate one for the situation at hand. To continue with the example above, it would be a much better practice for you to accept that you are primarily drawn to visual learning, and then bolster your capacity for auditory and kinesthetic learning (and so on), so you can better position yourself for learning based on content and context versus a habitual preference. This will, in turn, build your neural elasticity and allow you to more easily adapt to learning new things. Just remember: the content is the key to learning.

My suggestion for learning new skills is to work backward. Start by matching your learning strategy to the content you're studying instead of basing it on style. If you are trying to improve your reading skills, step one is simply to read more - and read correctly. Take your time to really understand the words you are reading, the syntax, the sentence structure, everything. This may appear tedious, but real learning is based on the content that you are studying, not an unsupported standard practice. You are pursuing an outcome, which means you want to start first with where you want to go, and then begin inching towards it incrementally.

Studies have also indicated that using your prior knowledge will help you learn new things. What you already know will have a strong effect on how well you can retain new information. When we connect new and old information, part of the brain associated with learning is activated. The implications of this are that learners can build stepping stones from what they know to what they don't yet, and that will improve and quicken their ability to take in new information. If you want to get better at reading, choose a subject you know fairly well or have some interest in. Did you play a sport in school? Do you like learning about different geographies? Choose a book you know will be "easier" for you to read so you can motivate yourself to stay the course with your learning.

Staying motivated will help keep you focused and committed to new learning. Learning based on what you are interested in is useful because it builds on what you want to do. It's a way of tricking yourself into really liking what you're learning. As with anything, the more fun we have doing it, the more likely we are to continue to do it.

Myth #2: Re-reading & Highlighting Will Help You Learn

Let's say you have an important meeting coming up. Is the first thing you do to refresh your memory on your talking points or re-read your materials? Do you have bullet points? Or maybe you memorize lines to share with the group. Whatever your approach is, you may be surprised to hear the statistics on what does and doesn't work.

Highlighting and underlining, in particular, have been found to be fairly ineffective learning strategies. Research indicates this approach is, in fact, a passive way of learning, and will likely not provide desired results. Passively reading the same text over and over again won't do anything for your comprehension or recall unless it's spaced out over time. While these practices are common, they offer very little benefit beyond what reading the text does. You must be actively engaged with the material.

Some research has even suggested that highlighting can interfere with learning because it distracts from the reader synthesizing connections and gaining a big-picture understanding by instead drawing attention to individual facts. Highlighting or underlining can also be detrimental if the wrong information is selected. Re-reading was also found to be ineffective at best, distracting and time-consuming at worst. Summarizing or writing down your ideas as you read was found to be more helpful than highlighting or underlining, depending on your relative skill level at doing so. Overall, all of these were deemed less useful exercises for learning by the scientific community.

Despite this, in a study conducted by Ulrich Boser, author of *Learn Better: Mastering the Skills for Success in Life, Business, and School, or How to Become an Expert In Just About Anything*, more than 80% of respondents believed that rereading is a highly effective approach to learning. Similar to broad beliefs on learning styles, public opinions on re-reading, highlighting, and underlining as a means of learning is more rooted in standard practice than it is in empirical evidence.

It's easy for us to assume we operate similar to computers because our brains serve as a kind of hard drive for our mental functioning. However, we are more than a database that collects various data points that flow past us. As humans, that's not how our learning works. Boser

9

found instead that learning is often a "form of mental doing" and supported more active, engaged methods of learning. We need to make sense of the content we seek to learn, so it can integrate within our mental systems as a wider understanding.

What To Do Instead

In contrast to more familiar practices like highlighting and re-reading, active learning strategies carry the most relevance and support, even if they aren't as well known. For instance, distributed study practice is a tactic that involves spreading out study sessions rather than engaging in one marathon, commonly referred to as 'cramming.' This may help you get through a meeting or test, but it will not stay with you as lasting learning. It is more effective to spread your learning out at intervals where you allow yourself to digest the material. Longer intervals mean longer-lasting learning.

In the shorter term, instead of re-reading, highlighting, or underlining important information, you can turn the information into a short quiz. This more active strategy will allow you to both process and integrate what you're learning. You can do this by asking yourself what the author is telling you at the end of every paragraph, in your own words. Summarize in the moment, and then compare it to what you already know. How is it similar to what you've read before? How is it different? How does it relate to other materials you've encountered on this subject? As you begin to make sense of what you're reading, you will deepen your learning potential.

Myth #3: Focus On One Subject At A Time

Historically speaking, we've been told it's good to practice one skill at a time. For instance, if you are a beginner pianist you may be told to rehearse scales before chords and to get one down before attempting to learn the other. If you're practicing a new sport, you may be told to break down learning based on one move at a time. In research terms, this is called blocking and is seen as common sense and easy to follow. It's also the dominant teaching practice in schools, professional training programs, and the likes.

Especially when it comes to learning a difficult subject, people widely believe you should practice one thing at a time. If you're learning to use a new suite of software, these people will suggest you practice one program one day and another the next, that way you can focus on fully understanding each one before moving on to something new. However, research shows you're more likely to confuse similar information if you study a lot of the same subject in one day like this. Blocking as a learning technique keeps you from distinguishing between two similar concepts.

Think about it. When you encounter a set of concepts (or terms or principles) that are similar in some way, you have a higher likelihood of confusing them with one another. You may mistake one word for another word with a similar spelling, or choose the wrong strategy for a math problem because they use a similar equation. You will make more errors more frequently when you expose yourself to only one main concept at a time.

11

What To Do Instead

An alternative approach is to expose yourself to different concepts by interleaving (or mixing) them together, so that one concept is followed by a different one. Learning related skills or concepts in parallel like this has been found to be a surprisingly effective way to train your brain. It's more effective to study multiple subjects each day than it is to do one deep-dive into a subject or two (especially if you're "cramming"). By mixing subjects, you are allowing your brain to have more time to consolidate new learning. Commonly called the "interleaving effect," this gives you a chance to see the core idea or big picture because, as you shift concepts, you gain a better sense of what each one means.

So, instead of a beginner pianist practicing only scales and then chords and then arpeggios (as with blocking), interleaving would involve alternating between practicing all of the above on a given day. Studies have shown this mixed method of learning tends to outperform blocking in a variety of subjects, from sports to categorical learning (such as math). Most recently, one study even found interleaving benefits critical thinking skills, as students who were trained with the technique were found to make more accurate assessments than those who used blocking techniques in complex learning scenarios.

The interleaving effect has also been found to have long-lasting effects on learning because it reinforces neural connections between different tasks and correct responses, which enhances your learning over time. This can often feel slow and difficult at the beginning, but what

12

this means is it can generate better long-term results. You have less likelihood of forgetting what you learn because it improves the brain's ability to discriminate between concepts through a series of practice attempts that are different from the last. In this way, automatic responses aren't applicable, as with blocking, where once you know what solution fits, or which move works, the learning is over and your brain disengages. Interleaving makes your brain consciously focus on finding the correct solution based on the context of the problem. This process can help you improve your ability to learn critical features of new skills and concepts, so that you can select and implement more appropriate responses.

Myth #4: The 10,000 Hour Rule

Journalist and author, Malcolm Gladwell, popularized the idea of the "10,000 hour rule," which states you need 10,000 hours of deliberate practice in order to become world-class in your chosen field. Recent research offers a counterpoint to this trend, however, suggesting that the amount of practice accumulated like this over time does not seem to play a major role in explaining individual differences in performance across all learning domains, including music, sports, and professional (or adult) education. Although practice is certainly essential when you're learning a new skill or studying a new topic, there's no magic number of hours that will turn you into an expert or bring you to the proficiency level of a professional athlete or musician.

In reality, practice alone doesn't make it perfect. What has been coined "deliberate practice" has been found to have less influence in

13

building expertise than previously thought. Researchers have studied deliberate practice as a means of understanding whether or not experts are "born" or "made" - or maybe a bit of both.

Overall, studies have found that deliberate practice is important, but not as important as advocates have claimed it is. There is a positive relationship between practice and performance, meaning the more people practiced, the higher their level of performance in a given domain. The difference is, the domain in question makes a difference in how well it effective it is. Deliberate practice is highly effective for games like Scrabble or chess, but less effective for sports, psychology, and related subjects.

What To Do Instead

The important question to consider moving forward is what else matters besides practice? Researchers at Princeton University point to the age a person begins an activity, along with individual variances in ability and commitment to learning as explanations for differences in human performance.

While researchers focus on determining why deliberate practice is not the answer, you can focus your attention on not convincing yourself there is a magic number to your success. Don't beat yourself up trying to meet an arbitrary number that may or may not actually help you reach your goal - and most likely will not. You won't become an expert this way, and you'll exhaust yourself in the process.

What works instead isn't just about time either; it's about seeking outside advice and input. Having this kind of feedback will be critical to your learning and will help keep you accountable. This is why hiring coaches or tutors can be so beneficial for your success.

Myth #5 You Are Either Right Or Left Brain Dominant

The idea that some people are right-brained while others are left-brained has been around for some time now. According to the theory, left-brained people are more logical, analytical, and methodical, while right-brained people are more creative and artistic. It is the basis for a myriad of personality tests, self-motivation books, and pseudo-psychology quizzes, and yet again this is not supported by any actual science. In reality, there are connections between all brain regions that enable humans to engage in both creative and analytical thinking; these things are not confined to only one side or another.

A recent study at the University of Utah has effectively debunked the myth through an analysis of more than one thousand brains. The study suggested that people do not typically prefer to use either their right or left side of the brain. Instead, they use their entire brain equally throughout the course of the entire experiment. We do prefer one side or the other - again, based on context. Scientists call this phenomenon "lateralization," or when we use one brain region more than others depending on the specific function required. For instance, speech comes from the left side of the brain for most right-handed people, but this doesn't imply that great writers or speakers use the left side of the brain more than the right, or that one side is bigger or richer in neural activity.

What To Do Instead

Don't divide yourself into one of these misleading categories. Understand that we all use our entire brain equally, and the fact that our brain is connected is what allows us to think both creatively and analytically, depending on what we are learning. Focus on how you can pursue the skills or expertise you've been meaning to conquer. Even if you tend to be more analytical than creative, or vice versa, this is not because you are relying too much (or too little) on a specific region of your brain. You aren't helping yourself by trying to fit into an existing (and incorrect) category of learner or thinker. What you want to do is enhance your learning in ways that will strengthen your ability to be flexible and to take in new information in longer-lasting ways.

Chapter Summary

Learning myths are extremely harmful in the way in which they have infiltrated into majority practice. The substance behind these beliefs is lacking and misleading for us as we approach learning new skills and subjects. Regardless of what you're trying to learn, you will need to come up with a strategy that works for you. You are regulating yourself, which means you have to set your own study rules. You are in charge of your own learning, so you will have to monitor your cognition, motivation, behavior, and learning environment in order to stay organized and focused. This process begins by knowing what not to do, which I have just covered. In the next chapter, you will learn key principles to prioritize that will accelerate your learning.

CHAPTER TWO

SEVEN KEY PRINCIPLES THAT OPTIMIZE THE LEARNING PROCESS

Learning something new may at first seem pretty difficult - and it can be. The good news is you can do something about it. You can improve your ability to learn by developing a good strategy that will work for you, and by following some basic guidelines that will help you accelerate your learning process.

Accelerated learning is not a new concept, and has been used by educators for decades now as a means of achieving a faster learning rate in students. To achieve desired learning outcomes in a shorter time frame (compared to conventional teaching practices), we have to first understand it is a holistic approach to learning. It integrates a mixture of teaching pedagogies and psychological theories to enhance and expedite learning. Perhaps most importantly is how it uses a learner's emotional and intellectual state as a basis for learning. It relies on intrinsic motivation to propel learning forward by focusing on learner needs, goals, life conditions, and so on, so that it truly offers a human-centric, practical approach to learning.

A leading expert in this methodology is Dave Meier, who wrote *The Accelerated Learning Handbook: A Creative Guide to Designing and*

Delivering Faster, More Effective Training Programs. Meier describes accelerated learning as the use of music, color, emotion, play, and creativity in a way that involves the whole person in their learning to enliven the entire experience. The principles overviewed in this chapter come directly from his comprehensive guide on learning new things more quickly.

I will focus on the seven leading principles that overview the highlights of Meier's handbook, so you will have a window into how your mind can acquire the knowledge you want. Each principle is derived from detailed studies on the human mind and leading methodologies of learning. You can use these principles to develop more substantial learning practices that will engage your whole brain and optimize your learning process. Once you understand these basic principles of accelerated learning, you will be able to properly implement them into your learning techniques.

Engage The Whole Mind & Body

Learning is not just in your mind; it is a combination of your body and your mind, and the connection between the two. This means you must use your whole self for learning: your mind, body, emotions, and all your senses. Science has shown us how using our entire brain is critical in order to make our learning faster, more interesting, and longer-lasting. The brain and body are inseparably connected. Moving your body, for example, can significantly improve your brain functioning, and certain brain states can have a profound effect on your body.

Your thinking, learning, and memory are not just all in your head, but are rather distributed throughout your body. In her book, *The Molecules of Emotion*, Candice Pert writes how much of our thinking, learning, and decision-making actually takes place on a cellular and molecular level. It is troubling, then, how we are almost always taught to separate our body from our mind. Traditional learning focuses on more conscious or rational, left-brained processes, or are strictly verbal. It tends to ignore the other senses by creating learning environments that do not engage the body, which would include our feelings and senses. In a learning context, moving our body helps stimulate chemicals essential for engaging our brain's neural network. This form of learning is referred to as "somatic learning" and denotes tactile, kinesthetic, or hands-on learning.

Somatic learners tend to be at a disadvantage in Western culture because our educational traditions tend to disregard the body as central to learning. We historically have told children to sit still and be attentive listeners in class instead of encouraging exploration, movement, and activity-based learning. There are many ways you can physically get your body involved in your learning; your learning doesn't have to be only, or even primarily, physical. It is, however, important to integrate some kind of body movement into your learning in a way where you alternate from physically active to physically passive learning.

Don't Just Consume - Create

Meier writes how knowledge isn't just something you absorb, but rather what you, as a learner, create. Learning happens when you fully integrate new knowledge by applying it in some way that makes it especially meaningful to you. You can make basic content more meaningful by creating a new significance for it that makes it relevant to you. This happens when you form new neural network connections and new patterns of interactions on a molecular level within yourself as you connect different concepts together. In turn, this will help you enforce a new work process or create a more practical application of newfound knowledge.

As you prepare yourself for learning, something you should do is take care to embrace a natural, more childlike state of wonder so that your innate ability to learn is engaged. This state is characterized by openness, freedom, fearlessness, joy, and curiosity. When you arouse your sense of curiosity, you open yourself up to new possibilities and connections; in essence, you make yourself fully ready to absorb and process new information. Learning, much like life itself, will stagnate if there is nothing left to be curious about or to engage with. Spark your curiosity by asking questions about the content you want to learn and you will find yourself learning and growing in ways you never imagined. If you approach your learning like a problem or a puzzle, you will engage your curiosity and find more motivation to learn.

You can also access and develop your sense of curiosity by using play as a means of engaging with learning content. When we have a sense of play, we release positive endorphins that bring us good feelings and help our bodies and minds engage in whatever it is we are trying to do. In terms of learning, this means we develop a creative intelligence that drives our ability to learn and grow.

Collaborate With Others

Traditional learning has created a tendency towards competition and individualistic learning that is steeped in isolation. Teaching pedagogies and universities have historically embraced individualism and the struggle to win, advance, versus a more tribal-based, collaborative approach to learning and interacting with others. Education has tended to emphasize individual achievement through individual grading that is strictly based on how students perform as everyone competes for the best grades. In theory, this was to create self-reliant individuals who work independently and in competition with one another as a motivating factor that educators hoped would lead to greater individual achievement. This over-emphasis on individualism in education, however, prevents the collective whole from being utilized to its fullest potential, which also means individual learners suffer. Isolation often creates an environment of stress and tends to reduce the speed and quality of learning. The competitive approach creates silos between learners instead of bridges from which information, intelligent, and real feedback is more readily possible.

Collaboration among learners enhances learning. Working with others engages us in a process of interaction that creates a social base and a network of support. This social base aids learning because, as humans, we are social learners. Collaboration between learners, such as learning through a learning community, creates space for individuals to really interact with each other and the content in a way that isn't distracted by hierarchy. Competition indicates there is a winner and a loser, whereas with collaboration there is a nurturing, understanding environment where learning can take place safely and openly. There is no longer a sense of competition between slower learners and faster learners, which inevitably creates avenues of cooperation that help speed up skill acquisition. It will help learners awaken their social intelligence when they collaborate, which researchers have found improves learning significantly.

Finding a genuine and collaborative learning community, where everyone can share their own particular experience or unique knowledge acquired, can work better as a learning tool rather than learning in isolation. If you have tried learning in isolation and felt drained, tired, or like you have mixed results, try collaborating with others who are also interested in your area of study and see what happens.

Learning Occurs On Many Levels, Simultaneously

Accelerated learning attempts to address the linearity of learning that comes from traditional teaching methods and the foundation of psychology. Behaviorism as a science seeks to explain human behavior in a systematic way, and yet it also has introduced a worldview of learning that is more mechanistic and disassociated rather than inclusive and interconnected. Modern formal education is based on learners as separate and disconnected which creates fragmentation to the learning process. Learning is divided into separate subjects, individuals are separate learners, and we as students are taught to learn one thing at a time.

Researchers have shown us, however, that learning isn't linear; rather, it involves absorbing many things at once. Effective learning engages you on many levels simultaneously: consciously, mentally, and physically. People take in knowledge with all of their senses and with their whole selves. We learn on many levels simultaneously. We have such a greater capacity for learning than has yet to be fully recognized on a wider scale by our methods of formal education. The rational consciousness of our minds is only part of our mental capacity; we utilize other cognitive functions such as verbal processing, creative imagining, and visual stimulation to aid our learning as well. The brain doesn't work in sequence; it processes information in a parallel way and thrives when it is challenged to do multiple things at once.

When you use multiple ways to learn something, you'll end up using more regions of your brain to store information about that subject. This makes information more interconnected and embedded in your brain, meaning it basically creates a redundancy of knowledge within your mind which helps you truly learn the information rather than only memorizing it.

Remember learning styles from Chapter One? Try mixing up different types of learning styles in order to absorb information in numerous ways. You can do this by using various kinds of media to stimulate different parts of the brain. For example, you can read notes, read a textbook, watch a video, and listen to a podcast (or audio file) on a given topic. The more resources (and variety) you use, the faster you'll learn.

Do The Work (With Feedback)

We know, unequivocally, that people learn best when content is rooted in real-world contexts. Contextual learning is non-linear, experiential, multi-layered, and uses the entire brain. Our brains are wired to digest entire contexts, not one isolated thing at a time. Non-contextual learning is piece-by-piece, fragmented and reminiscent of mechanistic thinking of the past. It would train us to have robotic responses in a narrow framework of learning, but would more often than not leave us feeling unfulfilled and lacking in abilities to think critically.

Lasting learning comes from doing the work itself, with feedback. Information that can be applied is far better than hypothetical constructs or abstract concepts. Facts or skills that are learned in isolation are harder to absorb and more quickly evaporate from memory. Doing the work itself provides the richest avenues for learning in a continual process of immersion, feedback, reflection, evaluation, and re-immersion. We will learn to sing by singing, how to swim by swimming, and so on. As learners, we need to immerse ourselves fully in a subject and to make it activity-based. Try and make it as authentic and based in real-world context as possible, because experience is the best feedback. It will enable you to learn on many levels, involve your whole brain (and body), and include the senses in your learning.

Think of ways you can create meaningful content relative to the subject matter you want to learn, and then deal with new learning material in a way that allows you to integrate it into your existing knowledge, skill-set, and sense of meaning. If you have the time and capabilities, you want to apply what you've learned. Find ways of getting quality feedback from trusted individuals, reflect on that feedback, and re-immerse yourself in your learning.

A quick word of warning against too much computer-use: computers tend to be isolating - albeit in some capacity helpful - learning machines. They are, overall, socially isolating devices that keep us separated from others and disengage us from collaborative learning. And again, as social creatures, people learn best not in isolation, but rather by interacting with others in a real-world context.

Be Positive

Studies have shown the effects of positivity, music, and involving play as a means to help people learn significantly faster and more effectively. The power of positive suggestion and supportive environments, in particular, cannot be understated. Our emotions, as verified through extensive research, have a profound effect on the quality of what and how we learn. Think back to some of your previous learning experiences, and you will probably be able to find examples of how this is true for you. Positive feelings are a catalyst for learning; feeling joyful as you learn new content will accelerate your learning. In contrast, negative feelings delay or even cease learning altogether. When feelings are positive and you are in a relaxed, open state, you will be able to access the higher levels of your brain. When your feelings are negative and you are stressed, you will tend towards using the shallower, more reptilian parts of your brain which are more dedicated to survival than complex cognitive processing. It is very difficult to learn in this state of mind.

Unfortunately, many people have negative feelings about learning. Perhaps they associate learning with memories involving previous pain, stress, humiliation, or other negative experiences. However, these negative suggestions (or assumptions) will have to be challenged with positive ones, or else learning will be stifled. Assumptions, in general, tend to color (or even create) our experience. Generally speaking, negative assumptions lead to negative experiences and vice versa.

As you approach learning new skills or subjects, it is then extremely important you focus on feeling positive. This doesn't mean an easy, superficial, or frivolous self-assurance. Real positive talk is essential and rooted in an honest, matter-of-fact attitude. Tell yourself what is good about what you're doing and why. What is valuable about what you are trying to learn? What will you be able to achieve after you have learned it? Be open and honest about your strengths and how they will help you accomplish your learning goals. As Meier puts it, "a positive feeling toward the learning experience is the necessary first step in learning." If you're feeling frustrated, stressed, uninterested, or bored, it's better for your learning if you take a break and return when you feel more motivated and positive.

It is also important to consider the environment in which you are learning. Much like your mental environment (or attitude) and your social environment (or collaborative learning scenario), your physical learning environment plays a role in how well you learn, and each of these factors feeds into one another. Think back to the various classrooms you've been exposed to. Did they inspire you to be there? Did they stimulate you to learn and grow? Traditional classrooms have historically been underwhelming at best. If your physical learning environment inspires negative feelings it can have an impact on your attitude, which will then affect how well you are able to integrate new information. Try - if you can - to create a space for your learning that you will want to occupy. This space should evoke feelings of curiosity, inspiration, and excitement. Doing so will help both relax and energize you for your learning.

Brains Love Visual Content

What Meier calls "the image brain" refers to the way in which our brains prefer visual stimulation because they absorb visual information instantly and automatically. Images are instantly memorable to us. Visual stimulation is easier for us to retain because it is concrete, whereas auditory and verbal stimulation tends to be more abstract. Think about it. You can probably recall, through imagery, thousands of your favorite (and least favorite) experiences. You can remember these so well not because you were concerned with memorizing them as they were happening; your image brain was doing it for you, in the moment, automatically and on many levels at the same time.

Studies have shown how courses that integrate imagery into classroom learning tend to produce students that have higher recall and long-term retention than courses that do not. Recall and retention rates were even higher in classrooms that used collaborative learning in addition to imagery to teach scientific content. This imagery can take a variety of forms, from graphics and other illustrations, to mnemonic devices or stories. In addition to these, you can always come up with your own creative method that works best for you.

Incorporating images into your learning is a natural way to teach yourself something faster and with higher quality. If you can translate verbal or auditory abstractions into concrete images of some kind, you will be more likely to retain that information and it will be easier for you to recall later. Words are important to us and integral to teaching; however, if you can associate words with images it will have a much more positive effect on your learning.

Chapter Summary

Remember: learning happens when you fully integrate new knowledge by applying it in some way that makes it especially meaningful to you. As learners, we need to fully exercise parts of our brains that emotionally connect us to new material for optimal performance. This means you must think critically as you navigate new information, decide how you want to approach your learning, and use your imagination to engage yourself in building these new skills. Therefore you want to: engage your entire body and mind; create rather than consume; collaborate with others; understand learning happens on several levels; do the work and seek feedback; have a positive outlook; and prioritize visual learning content. Doing this will ultimately help you to create more value out of the entire learning experience. Now that you have the principles you will need to consider your learning journey, the next chapter will focus on how you can structure your learning practice to more quickly acquire the skills you desire.

CHAPTER THREE

RAPIDLY (& PAINLESSLY) ACQUIRING NEW SKILLS

As you learn a new skill it may seem like the path to mastering it is long with many twists and turns. You may feel powerless at times, like it's useless for you to carry on trying. The good news is this is only as true as you allow it to be. There is a way you can learn a new skill quickly and effectively. Your brain tends to want you to master new things as quickly as possible, which can lead to frustration as you may want to skip the necessary steps to actually mastering it.

How fast you can develop a new skill depends first and foremost on your understanding of the stages of skill acquisition. If you understand the three learning stages of skill acquisition, you will be able to push yourself forward faster because you will be able to see where you are on your learning journey. As you progress, you will be able to map how you are doing more accurately. Everyone passes through these stages, so knowing which stage you are currently in will, in the end, actually help speed your learning along. It will save you lots of energy, frustration, and feelings of hopelessness. The three stages of skill acquisition sit on a continuum of skill learning, and move you from novice to expert. There is first the cognitive stage, then the associative stage, and finally, the autonomous stage.

The Cognitive Stage

The cognitive stage is usually characterized by frequent errors because it is a time when you as a learner have to think about the skill and how to execute it. As a learner, you are absorbed in mental processes associated with how you will gain this new skill. If you are an athlete, you will be thinking about your body position, which muscles to engage, and what each step of the skilled movement should look like. At each step, the learner will be fully focused on execution, which typically results in choppy movements that are incomplete. Imagine a child trying to learn a new motor movement. This is similar to adult learners attempting to improve a new motor skill: there is a lot of observation, attempts at mimicry, and likely frustration at their errors as they make mistakes. As such, this is a critical stage where the learner will benefit from frequent feedback. An instructor or coach will need to provide that feedback as well as demonstrations during the cognitive stage of skill acquisition. If you are teaching yourself, you will want to look for videos or other visualizations that will help show you what the skill looks like when it's well done. Break it down into various skill sections that you can gradually put together as you progress through your learning.

The Associative Stage

The associative stage of skill acquisition is the time when you as a learner have progressed from thinking about what you are doing to thinking about how you are doing it. This means you are no longer thinking about your body position and muscles, but rather where you are directing your movement. Where are you passing the ball? What's the end goal of your movement? You transition the focus from whether you can manage to do the movement you want to instead focus on what you want to achieve by doing so. During this stage, the movement becomes more fluid and smooth as the learner provides their own feedback instead of relying only on outside help. Most learners will still have errors as they continue along the skill acquisition continuum; however, these will not be as large or as frequent as during the cognitive stage of skill acquisition. As you progress through this stage, you will still benefit from immediate feedback on your performance and technique through a knowledgeable source. This will help you make critical adjustments and begin to increase the complexity of the context in which the skill is executed. For example, instead of hitting a tennis ball from a stable stand, you may have a partner hitting moving targets at you to return. From there, you will need a lot of frequent and large chunks of practice to move on to the autonomous stage.

The Autonomous Stage

The final stage, the autonomous stage of skill acquisition, is when you as the learner no longer think at all about the skill. In this stage, the movement comes naturally and is fluid and intuitive. You can now focus on other aspects of the skill movement, such as who to pass the ball to, where to move after the play, or think a few steps ahead of the current skilled motion. An autonomous athlete knows what the movement feels like and can consistently provide their own feedback. As with the previous stage, external feedback on skill execution will still be beneficial. Coaching an autonomous learner usually focuses on the execution of the skill under pressure and with various cognitive processes being completed simultaneously. This stage of skill acquisition is the mastery stage, and learners have characteristics such as kinaesthetic sense, good anticipation, consistency of performance, and sound technique. You will be able to correct your own movements, even midway through moving, as you adjust to oppositional movements or certain environmental interferences. You will be able to consistently perform the skill well with errors occurring very infrequently.

Now that you know a bit more about the three stages of skill acquisition, think back to something you've been meaning to learn - some new skill or talent. Maybe there are objects scattered about your house, anything from a textbook or that guitar you've been meaning to learn how to play. They may remind you of an abandoned potential project you were once so enthusiastic about that now you feel actual pain remembering how you gave up attempting to acquire it. Perhaps you've even tried again, only to fail yet again.

When you consider the stages of skill acquisition above, you have to understand you have never moved through the most painful ones: the cognitive and the associative stages. You're still a newbie so you've gotten stuck in committing errors and as a result, you have given up. Your brain is actually designed to protect you from pain during the first two stages. It wants to just skip ahead to the autonomous stage right

34

away where you've already mastered the skill, or at least where your skills have plateaued. Keep in mind, this is all about leaving your comfort zone. You're stretching yourself beyond what you're used to, so hang in there. You're still in these earlier stages of learning, and you can avoid some of the growing pains.

Time is such a valuable resource for all of us, so I've included some of the leading research on rapid skill acquisition. Josh Kaufman has outlined key principles on how to do this in his book *The First 20 Hours* (we'll return to this concept in the next chapter). The following six recommendations will help you learn the basics of anything in less time. Here's how you get there.

Choose a Passion Project

Think about what you are most passionate about. What gives you a sense of meaning? Is it designing for accessibility? Becoming a great leader? Where do you find pleasure? Is it giving customers a great experience? Providing excellent products? Acquiring skills rapidly is all about finding and developing new strengths by leaving your comfort zone, so if you are trying to learn a new skill, you must leave your comfort zone. This means you leave your old strengths behind as you focus on growing new ones. As you choose a project you are passionate about, ask yourself where you find meaning in your life and what activities give you pleasure. Build out a visual that will help you pinpoint these necessary ingredients. You can even map out where your current strengths are so you have an accurate picture of what you would like to further develop.

35

When we pick something we're interested in, we'll have the discipline to push through the cognitive and associative stages of skill acquisition, to put forth the necessary time and effort to acquire the skill, and to reach the finish line. Once you know why you're passionate about this project that you love, you can plan around it. Set goals for your success. Research and acquire the proper equipment and resources you will need for your learning journey. Then, plan your schedule around this chosen path. Get organized and pumped for the path ahead.

Focus Your Efforts on One Skill at a Time

You only have so many hours in a day, and learning a new skill can be difficult. If you try to divide your limited time and cognitive resources across learning a variety of skills, you will likely burn out; unfortunately, burnouts do not learn very quickly. When the world moved at a slower pace, multitasking was a valuable skill to claim. Nowadays, however, it has been proven to make you a less effective individual and a less efficient learner. If you try to do two or more tasks at once, it will actually decrease your productivity by forty percent. Remember, just as you should avoid multitasking at work, you should absolutely avoid it as you dedicate yourself to learning a new skill. You need to immerse yourself in your skill acquisition process so you can reach your skill potential.

There are likely many different skills you'd like to acquire, but an important first step of rapid skill acquisition is for you to choose one to focus on first. Start by making a list of all the skills you're interested in, and then pick the one that is most exciting to you right now. This excitement will help you stay motivated through your practice. Though it may be tempting to try and dive into several skills at once, you should focus all of your energy on learning a single skill at a time. For instance, you may have been tempted to combine learning Python coding with learning Spanish, search engine marketing, and video editing. Studies have shown this is not how you will gain a new skill the fastest. You must use your time wisely when trying to learn something new since you may only have about an hour each day to dedicate to it. Try not to try to learn multiple new things at once, because you'll progress much more slowly, which will in turn not help motivate you to continue.

Decide Your Target Performance Level

How skilled at this do you truly want to be? Once you've decided you are obsessed with learning this new skill, you will now have to decide just how much being great at it matters to you - and how great you want to be. Do you want to be an upper echelon master, or do you want to just be pretty good? For intense competitors, the answer will always be "I want to be the best," but it's completely alright to know the basics and stick in the middle if it's just a hobby to you. If you want to take up soccer mostly to socialize and know you can hold your own on the field, then great. This principle is completely up to your preference and where you want to be.

Break Your Skill into Sub-skills

Begin with setting and mastering sub-skills that you can build upon. This will help you begin to visualize your learning success. Planning is critical as you do this because if you have no path or vision for what your success looks like, you will be stuck in the preliminary principles wondering when you'll figure it out. A new skill is rarely one thing to achieve. There are tactics you can use to break it down, deconstruct the skill you're trying to learn into separate parts. You can then order those parts in a way that will allow you to accomplish your target performance as quickly as possible.

Provide Proper Tools to Optimize Your Skill

Sometimes when we're learning something new, we throw ourselves into the ring without doing the proper research. If you want to learn a new language, chances are you won't find the best resources that will help you do so for free. If you really want to learn how to play the guitar, you're definitely going to need a guitar and, most likely, guitar lessons. This means you should be sure you budget your process just as you would with any other important life decision. You want to make sure you have the right tools with you for your success. What will you need at each step to get there? Alternatively, what will get in your way, or serve as a barrier to your learning? Identify the necessary resources and potential obstacles you may encounter.

Quantity over quality

In my opinion, this is the most important principle for learning new skills as quickly as possible. We've been told time and time again to focus on "quality over quantity," and that may be true in some circumstances, like when it comes to having friends or buying fewer items. With rapid skill acquisition though, it's the exact opposite. Before you enter every learning session you have to understand that you are not an expert, and won't be for a little while. You will have to work on being less critical about your performance from session to session. You have to realize that you are slowly progressing. Practice as much as you can with consistent feedback. Keep yourself motivated and engaged. Plan your practice schedule out so that you have dedicated time for what you need to do. This will force you to put in the hours necessary to achieve your target performance goals. Try also practicing at the same time for consistency, as this will help you actually keep with it.

Chapter Summary

Now you know the three stages of skill acquisition (cognitive, associative, and autonomous) and my key recommendations on how to learn the basics of anything new in less time. These are: choosing a passion project to give you greater discipline and motivation; focusing your efforts on one skill at a time to reach your full learning potential; deciding your target performance so you have realistic learning expectations; breaking your skill down into sub-skills so it's more attainable; identifying proper tools for your success, and obstacles to it; and lastly, practicing as much as you can with consistent feedback. If you prioritize learning a new skill using these points as a guide, you will be on your way to success. In the next chapter, you will learn how best to approach your first - and most important - twenty hours of your learning.

CHAPTER FOUR

THE FIRST TWENTY HOURS

As previously mentioned, Josh Kaufman is a noted rapid learning expert who has suggested twenty hours as a magic number for learning a new skill. The six principles I just overviewed are critical for a new learner to consider throughout this twenty-hour learning journey. According to Kaufman, everyone will hit a wall early on in the rapid learning stage, so by pre-committing to twenty hours new learners will have a sure-fire way to push through that wall to acquire a new skill. This won't necessarily mean you become an instant master at a new skill, but rather that you will reach a higher competency level more quickly and more surely.

The first few hours of learning something new are always the hardest, and this is where the majority of people give up. It's essential, however, to continue to push through the first twenty hours of practice, regardless of whatever bumps in the road you may run into. Once you get through the first twenty hours, you'll have a significant amount of practice under your belt, so subsequent practice will not be as difficult. Here are my recommendations for how to approach your first twenty hours of practicing a new skill.

Start by Setting Your Goal

First, decide what skill level you want to achieve. I briefly talked about setting your target performance level in the last chapter. Now really consider where you want to be and how you want to get there. One key idea of *The First 20 Hours* is to begin by deciding how good you want to become at a skill. Once you have an idea of the skill level you are eyeing to achieve, then you will break it down into smaller steps to reach it.

For example, say you want to become good at marketing copywriting because you need to write an email to land a deal with a high-ticket potential client. You don't need to extensively study copywriting in its entirety. You can look at the best practices for writing sales emails, instead. You can figure out the steps and bite-sized pieces that you will need to write that perfect email for your use in this scenario. Make a plan. Begin by first studying how to write subject lines, then how to properly personalize your emails, and finally the proper tone and voice, maybe even suggestions on how to avoid landing in the spam folder, and perhaps some principles of influence to ensure that your email converts. You can also research different templates that you can then tailor to your use, and so on.

Keep in mind, with the right goal set you're more likely to succeed in acquiring the skill you've set your sights on. It may help with your accountability if you share your goal with a friend. Having a social implication for your learning will help keep you motivated along the path to achieving your goal. There are also huge benefits to learning in a group. Remember collaborative learning? When you learn in a group, not only are you able to learn from others, but you'll also be encouraged to make progress together. Whether it is a chess club, a mastermind group, or an online meet-up group, try to connect with other like-minded individuals, if nothing else for feedback and support.

Decide What Resources You Need

Since we're talking about learning a new skill within twenty hours, it's important to decide what you will need to get you started. How can you stay focused? You will have to work to limit distractions and make sure that you have the tools you need to learn and succeed at your desired skill. While it may seem like a simple step, it is of utmost importance for you to do carefully and correctly. Begin by figuring out what types of materials and environments - even tools or apps - will be able to support you in your success in learning this new skill. Perhaps you simply need a pen, paper, and highlighter for marking passages in textbooks. Or maybe you'd rather automate your learning sessions by gathering online references and reading them on your mobile tablet. Alternatively, maybe you prefer learning in wide open spaces, such as outdoors or in a park, or maybe you prefer learning in the comforts of your own home, listening to music or next to your favorite window.

As you make sure the environment you are in is perfect for your rapid-learning progress, you have to take care to ditch any social media or related distractions, including the temptation to check messages or emails. As the saying goes, "out of sight, out of mind." Before you sit down to practice or study, make sure all potential distractions are far from sight. You can plan ahead by setting a specific place for learning that doesn't have a TV, talkative friends, or other temptations. Taking control of your environment like this also doesn't necessarily mean you always need to do it alone. Sometimes working with friends in study groups can be a useful way to influence your environment.

Once you have your ideal environment down, you can move on to identifying potential barriers or roadblocks that may interfere with your learning process and work to eliminate them. You want to create a distraction-free environment so you can focus on your learning. Remember how your brain will look for shortcuts, and any excuse to not practice. It will try to turn back at any barrier because you are in the early stages of learning, which can be painful. You have to work to remove these barriers. If you're learning how to play the guitar, leave it in the middle of your room so you constantly see it and are reminded of your commitment to practice. You want it to be as obtrusive a reminder as possible so you can't avoid it.

You should also try to anticipate emotional roadblocks as well. For instance, maybe you are beginning to feel overwhelmed or anxious. Remember how having a positive attitude aids your learning process? Take a break if you find yourself struggling to feel optimistic and relaxed, and then return to your process when you have a renewed sense of motivation to learn. This is not the same as commitment. You have to make yourself power through the first twenty hours, according to this theory, so you have a higher likelihood of acquiring your new skill.

Sometimes that means committing to even the smallest amount of work even when your motivation is lacking.

Practice, Practice, Practice

When planning your skill acquisition process, you have to make sure to allot time for practice. In order to become an expert, there is no substitute for this. It takes dedication, discipline, and focus, as well as a sincere, genuine desire to do the work. If you aren't passionate about something, you won't become an expert at it. You must stay consistent, or you'll backtrack. Ideally, you will practice or study at the same time every day. If you're struggling on how to make time for this, start by cutting out any other activities that aren't directly necessary to learning this new skill. Fill that time with practicing.

Obviously, you can't completely clear your schedule like this; there are adult responsibilities you have to do and emergencies that arise day-to-day and week-to-week. However, if you're serious about learning a new skill, cut out most of the fluff in your schedule and re-dedicate it to this. Your goal is to free up sixty to ninety minutes a day to dedicate to practicing. Don't forget to receive feedback on your progress so you can find out whether you've gone wrong anywhere, or if you should be approaching your learning in a different way. Feedback is critical in the early stages of skill acquisition. You may even want to hire a coach to help you with this. Coaches can guide you and give you feedback throughout the process in ways that may be difficult for you to do yourself. In some instances, you can monitor your own learning. For example, if you're learning a new language, you could try using a voice recorder to listen to yourself speaking. This will make it easier for you to hear mistakes in your pronunciation or grammar.

It can be easy to get caught up in reading and gathering information on how to do something and never actually get around to doing it. Just remember: the best way to learn how to do something is to actually do it. Regardless of how unprepared you may feel, make sure you are continually physically or actively engaged. Keep yourself alternating between research and practice, with lots of practice in between research stints.

Practice in Short Bursts

If you're like me, you dread the end of the weekend. The workweek looms ahead on Sunday night, promising to bring endless new tasks to complete. If you're learning a new task, this can be even more daunting. The good news is there's a better way for us to approach these long periods of work without feeling overwhelmed. Learning something new that is difficult, or even working on activities for long periods of time, is draining and often inefficient. Research has found that it's actually better to work in short bursts with frequent planned breaks. This is commonly referred to as the Pomodoro Technique.

The Pomodoro Technique calls for us to take a five-minute break after every twenty-five minutes of work. Set session goals so you accomplish three to five of these work sessions throughout your day. Once you do this, you'll be amazed at how quickly you progress. By prioritizing quantity and speed, you're much less likely to get frustrated - and as a result, demotivated - during your initial stages of practice.

When you first start to learn something new, the hours of practice it takes to really start making progress can feel like an eternity. You may even think you've spent more time working on something at the beginning of learning a new skill, just by how hard the learning task itself is. Using the Pomodoro Technique will help you avoid frustrations as you begin your learning process. It will help keep you focused and motivated, as you'll be able to track your time working.

When you work on a task without a break, you're more likely to lose focus and as a result, get sidetracked from doing real work. When you take a break, however, you force yourself to have a few seconds to re-evaluate or reflect on your work. You give yourself the necessary space so your attention can rest before returning to your task. You may find that you need to adjust what you're working on, or make some necessary change. It will increase the quality of your work as well as the speed at which you're able to do it. When it's time for your break, it's important for you to take it seriously and really move to a new activity. You can treat them as a reward for your hard work where you walk a bit, do some stretches, grab a cup of coffee, or do something that relaxes you (like meditation). You can experiment with how long you prefer to work before you take a break, although research tends to suggest that somewhere between twenty-five and thirty-five minutes is the sweetest spot. Keep in mind that longer work periods can lead to burnout, which is especially harmful for your motivation if you're trying to learn a new skill.

Kaufman also suggests that you practice your new skill within four hours of going to sleep. According to him, practice done within this timeframe causes your brain to integrate the learning more rapidly into your brain's neural pathways because your memory and the motor-mechanics needed are ingrained at a quicker level. You can also help your brain by celebrating the little wins along the way. This will result in more endorphins and serotonin released which will, in turn, encourage you to continue. Have a piece of chocolate or watch one of your favorite music videos as a treat so you keep having fun. Learning a new skill should be exciting and something you cannot wait to practice every day. Keep your good attitude and motivation strong!

Chapter Summary

Inspired by learning expert, Josh Kaufman, this chapter covered how you can structure your first twenty hours of learning a new skill. Remember that by pre-committing to twenty hours, you will have a way to push through the learning wall everyone experiences and achieve your learning goals. My four key recommendations for how you can approach the first twenty hours of your learning are to: start by setting your goal; decide what resources you need to succeed; consistently practice and seek feedback early on; and finally, break your practice periods down into digestible intervals so you don't lose your motivation. All of these work together in a way that will increase the quality and efficiency of your learning. In the next chapter, you will learn about my all-time favorite learning principle and how it can serve you on your learning journey.

CHAPTER FIVE

THE LIFE-CHANGING PARETO PRINCIPLE

You may have never heard of the Pareto Principle, but you have most likely heard of the eighty-twenty rule or the law of the vital few. The Pareto Principle suggests that, for most things, approximately eighty percent of the effects come from twenty percent of the causes. This has been applied to everything from land ownership, to taxation, to mathematics. This rule is based on a power law distribution and has been proven true in business, in relationships, and most importantly, in how we learn. In terms of learning, it means that you want to identify the twenty percent of work (or causes) that will give you the eighty percent of results you want (the effects). The main concept lies in identifying the few most effective strategies and materials that will allow you to quickly become adequate in the chosen subject.

For example, if you're learning a language, it does not take long to realize there are a few key words that tend to pop up over and over again. You can do a quick search for "most commonly used French words" or "typical French phrases" to begin to learn how to speak French before going into the more technical or grammatical details. When applied to athletic training, you can use the Pareto Principle by practicing around twenty percent of the key exercises and habits for a particular skill in order to have eighty percent of the impact. The learner should not focus so much on a varied training or learning very technical aspects of a skill. It's basically telling you what to start with first - not that the other eighty percent doesn't matter. For instance, having a healthy diet and going to the gym regularly are still important for athletic training, but they are not as significant as the key (or twenty percent) activities.

The Pareto Principle will change the way you learn. Depending on your chosen skill, the amount of study material can be immense. You will need a strategy to choose the most effective material that will help you achieve your goal, as well as put it in the right sequence. Applying this principle to your learning can be done in various ways. You can use it to choose the most effective approach for studying that is available to you. Beyond studying methods, the eighty-twenty rule can be extremely useful in choosing the right material. I've compiled some helpful tips for you to consider as you use this approach to rapidly acquire a new skill.

To begin with, identify the skill that you are currently trying to learn. It doesn't matter if it's a sport, a language, a motor skill (like playing the guitar or another kind of instrument), or learning a new game (such as chess). No matter which field, skill, or expertise, just choose something you are trying to improve in. It could even be a new task that's been recently assigned to you by your boss or a teacher. It could be a new specialization or hobby. Identify the learning subjects in your life and be open to discovering more than one simultaneously.

Compiling this list will help you organize yourself in your learning process.

Now make a list of the five to ten resources you use in your learning process. For each of the topics or skills you've thought of, now you want to consider five or more things you are currently doing in your learning with each one, or that you are actively working on improving. For instance, if one of the skills you are trying to learn is how to play guitar, list out five or more actions you are taking to help your learning. These can also be resources you are using that are helping you improve.

Once you've done this, you can choose the one or two items that provide you with the best results. Choose carefully and as unbiasedly as possible. Even if it's something that you find difficult or to be somewhat of a struggle, if it's helping your learning, it goes on the list. Remember that the goal at this point is not to get to mastery, but rather getting to your eighty percent as quickly as possible. Excitement and motivation will help you go on from there. In addition, you will now be more familiar with the subject and will be able to make more educated decisions from here on out. After you choose the two items that will provide you with a quicker fluency, you will be in a much better position to incrementally learn more and learn faster. If nothing on your list fits this description, head back to the beginning of your resource list and add some new ones. It may take some trial and error at first, but don't worry! Reach out for feedback from a trusted friend or mentor or do a quick Google search if you need to. We live in an era of information. Everything you need is at your fingertips.

The final step in applying the Pareto Principle is to practice the two items you've chosen to be the most effective and efficient in providing you with your results for the next two weeks. You've done your process of elimination, now it's time to practice. You will see, over the course of this practice session, how much further along you come than you may have initially expected. You can also apply the Pomodoro Technique and keep in mind the stages of skills acquisition as you do this phase as well. All of these principles play together in a way that will both deepen and quicken your learning.

Beyond learning, you can use the Pareto Principle in any area of your life where you feel there may be an imbalance of effects. It may not be applicable to all areas, but many situations you may find are out of balance (for instance, financial, health, marital, social, or professional). You can think of the top ten to twenty percent of inputs you put into your life on the whole to get eighty percent of what you want out of life. Maybe you'll discover you value relationships more than you thought; maybe it will improve an aspect of your professional life.

You can then find ways to emphasize the key percentage that brings you that eighty percent of joy or satisfaction. Decide to spend more time in those activities and place them first in your schedule. Maybe you meet with more of your key friends or reinstate date night into your relationship. Or maybe it's investing more of your money in the experiences you want to have. You will also want to find ways to downplay or eliminate the rest of the activities that don't give you the same payoffs. This may mean you cut some toxic people out of your life, or redirect your money to smarter or better investments that have better results and give you an overall higher quality of life. Whatever the case, the eighty-twenty rule can be a guiding light for you in overall creating more balance for your day-to-day.

Chapter Summary

The Pareto Principle is my favorite learning principle. It serves you by helping you identify the twenty percent of work that will give you eighty percent of the results you want. Learning this is truly life-changing. It will help you prioritize the most effective learning strategies and materials that will guide you towards your learning outcomes. You can use this amazing tool in other areas of your life as well to find more overall balance. In the next chapter, I'll give you an overview of key points to consider in the art of effective note-taking.

CHAPTER SIX

THE ART OF EFFECTIVE NOTE TAKING

Research on memory has indicated that we easily remember ideas or information that we turn our attention to often, and conversely how we can quickly forget the ideas or information that we mentally touch only once or twice. This is intentional and developed as humans evolved. It's a natural forgetfulness of information because our brains are filtering out the data we're telling it isn't important. It's simple: the less we expose ourselves to something, the less we will retain it in our minds. We tell our minds what's important to keep by introducing it and reintroducing it into our days through practice and study. The more we practice, the more permanently information is stored in our minds.

When we try to learn something new, our recall is strongest right off the bat. Imagine you're studying vocabulary in class, and you're introduced to twenty new terms. If you were tested immediately, you would likely have a recall of near one hundred percent. One day later, your recall would be down by forty percent. As learners, if we don't return our attention to new material, within the first twenty-four hours we will have lost forty percent of that information. Even one day later, and we lose another twenty percent of recall ability. So in two days, we will have forgotten sixty percent of our new learning. This effect is called the "forgetting curve" and was developed by Herman Ebbinghaus in 1895 as he conducted early research on memory and forgetfulness.

In short, our temporary memory can be deceiving. We hear something and we think because we can immediately think about and repeat it that we will remember it later as well. Think of it like this. Our brains have attached a drop of glue to a thought (as temporary memory). Gradually the glue loses its adhesive quality, and because it was only a drop, the bond disperses and we no longer remember the thought. However, if we constantly return to that one thought, and apply additional drops of glue to the original drop, the adhesive is strengthened over time. Eventually, the information will become part of more permanent memory.

Because information is lost quickly over time, learners need to develop an effective strategy to retain new information. Note-taking is a good tool to help with this; however, just plain taking notes will not be enough to do the trick. Effective note-taking is designed to help you recall what you have learned and to retain that information well over time. If we take notes effectively we can retain and retrieve almost 100% of what we learn.

How To Take Notes

One easy place to start is to always write your notes by hand. Although it might seem like typing your notes on a laptop during a conference or lecture would be more thorough (and maybe even help you learn faster) the opposite is in fact true. It is better for your learning if you take notes with a pen and a piece of paper. Doing so will both

56

speed up your learning as well as help you to retain it. Research has shown that learners who type their lecture notes process and retain the information at a lower level. Those who take notes by hand in contrast actually end up learning more.

While taking notes by hand is slower and more cumbersome than typing, the act of writing the information fosters higher levels of comprehension and retention. Reframing the information in your own words helps you retain the information longer, meaning you'll have better recall and will perform better on tests. This happens because we have different types of cognitive processing associated with taking notes by hand versus typing. When typing, learners can easily produce a written record of the lecture without necessarily processing its meaning. Faster typing speeds allow students to transcribe a lecture word for word without putting much thought into the content or deeper meaning behind what was said. Because learners can't write down everything they hear by hand, they have to make choices on what to prioritize and focus on. You will have to instead listen, digest, and summarize what you're hearing so that you can succinctly capture the essence of the information. Taking notes the old-fashioned way forces the brain to engage in heavier mental lifting than if you were typing, and these efforts then lead to higher rates of longer-lasting learning.

Studies on taking notes have found note-taking is more effective when they are organized and transformed in some way, or when a teacher gives examples of how to take good notes on the given material. Either way, it requires effort, and half the battle is understanding the reasons for needing to take and interact with notes. The most effective note-taking skills involve active as opposed to passive learning, which means the responsibility for learning is placed on the learner. Research has shown how actively involving and engaging students in the process of learning is critical for lasting learning. Despite these findings, traditional classrooms tend to mostly encompass listening to formal presentations versus reading, writing, discussing, solving problems, or otherwise engaging with the learning material. What's important to note about this form of learning is that it involves higher-order thinking tasks such as analysis, synthesis, and evaluation.

These learning strategies promote active learning because they involve the learner in learning things and then actively thinking about what they are doing as they are doing it. This is commonly referred to as thinking about thinking, or metacognition. While learners are engaging with their content, they should also be considering how they are learning it, what works, what causes confusion, and how the thinking changes as the topic of learning changes. This will help you as a learner discover what is working well for you, and what adjustments you should make next time. It will help you learn from your mistakes faster and more effectively. Metacognitive practices will also increase your overall ability to transfer and adapt your learning to new contexts and tasks.

In regards to note-taking, these concepts have several implications. It's an interactive process and involves using the original notes many times over in order to build a memory of the content, as opposed to just assuming taking notes is a one-time copying activity. One leading strategy for note-taking is called the Cornell Method, which provides a guide for taking notes that will help you organize your notes into more easily digestible summaries. This method outlines four stages of good note-taking.

#1 Note Taking

To begin with, you will want to prepare a page to take notes and do so the same way each time. Write an essential question at the top of the page that is relevant to the topic of study to focus on a key learning objective that you should be able to discuss after your study session. You can then divide the page into columns. One will take up around a third of the page and will be left blank for questions and related notes that can be added later when the notes are revisited. The other side is for notes captured during a conference, lecture, or learning session (this can include notes from a textbook, video, podcast, or related source as well).

Throughout the learning session, you want to listen and take notes in your own words rather than writing down verbatim what you hear or see. Paraphrase what you're hearing so it makes sense to you. You can leave spaces in your notebook between main ideas so you can return to it later and add information. As you listen, make sure to write in phrases rather than complete sentences (using bullet points and lists where possible), and develop your own consistent style of abbreviations or symbols to save you time. As you engage with the learning content, you will get better at how you can listen for important information versus trivial information. It will help you to take cues from the instructor or source. If it says this is critical or a key theme, that's a sign for you to pay extra attention to what follows. Finally, you can use highlighters or colored pens or pencils as you take notes to indicate key changes in ideas, concepts, or any links between information. Getting creative like this will also keep you better focused and on task because you will be finding ways to stay interested and engaged in the content.

#2 Note Making

Now revisit your notes and revise the content. Review what you've written and see if there's anything you need to edit or adjust for accuracy or clarity. Write questions in the column you left blank from before that correspond with the answer (your original notes) on the other side. Use highlighters or symbols to connect key chunks of information or material together in a cohesive way. This is also a good time for you to seek feedback. You can exchange ideas and collaborate with other learners, or even better, an instructor or coach, so you can check your understanding and test the comprehensiveness and correctness of your notes.

#3 Note Interacting

Once you have reshaped your notes, now you want to link all your learning together by writing a summary that addresses the essential question, and that answers the questions you wrote in the column during your note-making. Remember that a summary is a general overview of the content you are learning, which is different than a reflection that instead focuses on your response to the learning task or content. You can learn from your notes by building in regular times for revising your notes for each topic of study you have. When you return to study them later, you can use the questions and answers to quiz yourself.

#4 Note Reflecting

The final stage of note-taking incorporates reflection on the content you have written down. You should seek out written feedback from a peer, tutor, or instructor to check for your comprehension and accuracy as it is still the initial learning phase. You should then should address the feedback by focusing on one area of challenge you are experiencing in their learning that is related to this content, and any questions that arise from it. This will help you deepen your overall understanding of the content in the long run. As a learning tool, reflection is helpful to do periodically throughout the entire learning process, especially leading up to major exams, presentations, or other performance measures.

Additional Study Tips

As with many things, note-taking is only the first step in your study process, so I want to close this chapter with a few additional helpful tips that you can use once you have your notes at the ready. In general, keep in mind the more times you touch new information, the less you will forget it.

1. **Study in a Question/Answer Format.** Whether you are reading a textbook chapter or going over your lecture notes, try to always be looking for an answer to a salient question you have created to focus your attention on deepening your understanding of the content. Oftentimes the format of a test is in question/answer, so you're also priming yourself for important benchmarks on your

performance. You will be learning the information in the way a test will likely ask it.

2. **Use Flashcards When Applicable.** Use your notes as a guide, and then put any information you can on flashcards: a term, a question, etc, on the front of the card, and the definition or answer on the back. Remember, only one idea, term, or question per card. This is another way for you to use the question/answer format. Flashcards are also very portable. You can take them with you everywhere and use any spare five to ten minutes here and there each day to quiz yourself.

3. **Study in Small Chunks.** The best way to learn something well is to introduce it gradually into your mind in brief intervals over a period of time. This is the opposite of cramming, when you try to absorb large amounts of information in one or two long sessions. Cramming is the least effective study method for long-term retention; however, as I'll discuss later, there is a place for it in rapid skill acquisition. In general, you will retain information better if you break your study session down into four or five ten-minute study periods. If you do this every day learning up to a performance review, you will do very well.

4. **Make a Schedule.** It will help to have a study plan and for you to study according to your priorities. You want to decide how you want to divide your study sessions and organize your time. It may be worthwhile to keep a calendar of tests and assignments (either that you're assigned or that you make for yourself). Study

and schedule your learning periods for when you are most alert. If your life allows you, give yourself breaks between learning new content and going to work or moving on to another activity. These breaks will allow you to review what you've just learned and even potentially preview what you're going to do or learn next (if applicable).

5. **Distribute and Modify Your Practice.** Research has found that it's better to use short study sessions to learn a topic over a period of time. This will encourage meaningful learning that is longer lasting. The more you space out your practice sessions the more effective they will be over time. It will help you retain the information and stay motivated to keep learning. Additionally, making slight changes during these repeated practice sessions will help you master a skill faster than if you did it the same way each time. This only works if the modifications you make are small. Big changes in practicing a new skill won't help in the same way.

Chapter Summary

When taking notes, prioritizing a few simple things will go a long way. Take notes by hand because the act of writing out the information fosters higher levels of comprehension and retention. Reframing information in your own words will also help you retain the information longer, meaning you'll have better recall and will perform better on tests. Note-taking is also an interactive process, and involves using original notes many times over utilizing a process called the Cornell

Method (note-taking, note-making, note-interacting, and note-reflecting). Besides the Cornell Method, I also gave you a few additional study tips to consider as you structure your learning sessions, such as: studying in a question and answer format; using flashcards; studying in small chunks; making a schedule; and distributing and modifying your practice. In the next chapter, you will learn how to take your learning one step further and accelerate your expertise.

CHAPTER SEVEN

HOW TO ACCELERATE YOUR EXPERTISE

When you're new to learning something, it can be tricky as you work to upgrade from moderately skilled into the level of expert. You've started from a basic level, and depending on how steep the learning curve is for your given topic, it may take a little while for you to get where you want to be. For starters, you'll want to get in the right mental shape. Prepare yourself mentally and have a good attitude. It will be challenging, but with the right help, you can get there quickly and surely.

With the incredible rise in technology these days, rapid learning is more of a reality than we realize. This generation of learners lives in the age of knowledge and information. Just think: through the internet, we are able to access all kinds of knowledge so we can answer almost any conceivable question we may have. What's more, is the notion of people being natural-born geniuses or savants is constantly being questioned and replaced by research that suggests we are much more naturally programmed to learn. All we need is the right guidance so you can figure out your own unique code for learning. The following recommendations will help you discover this, as well as stay on the right track in quickly becoming an expert in your chosen field.

Find a Mentor

Remember: success leaves clues. The best shortcut to becoming an expert is to find an expert who already does what you want to achieve, and then form a relationship with them so you can learn from their story. This is as much about the failures as it is about the successes. You want to try and not make the same mistakes that your mentor has made on their road to success. Finding out what not to do from the expert will fast-track your learning of a new skill. It will be a huge win to have this person more personally walk you through what needs to be done.

Many people misunderstand how to approach finding a mentor. You may want one but not quite understand what it even means. You'll want to really do your research and select a couple of candidates you'd like to have as a mentor. Take a minute to consider a few things before reaching out to them. Chances are this person is a leader whom you admire, and the way in which you approach them could be the make or break in whether or not they accept your invitation. The last thing you want to do is to put someone in an awkward position where they may feel bad for saying no or obligated to say yes.

Remember first and foremost that mentoring is not all about you. The person you want as your mentor will likely also not be looking for you, so you have to assume an active attitude to your approach. Really consider what you want from this person. They should be someone you want to be like, not just someone who has a job that you want. This person should have a similar set of strengths and skills that you want to adopt and learn from. Having several candidates isn't a bad idea before you decide to commit to one (or two, depending on your availability). Once you've selected who you'd like to have as a mentor, get to know them. Read articles they've written, follow their blog, and so on. The more you know about this person and their public persona, the more realistically you'll be able to set your expectations.

Now that you've done your research, you're ready to make the ask. Try not to mention the word 'mentor' right off the bat. It's a little bit of a tall order for a first meeting. Instead, ask for an initial meeting, and personalize your message with something that drew you to them in the first place. Don't go for flattery, just be honest and insightful. Maybe you read an article or a quote from them, or you are a fan of the organization they work for. Then choose a place that's informal, like a coffee shop, and keep the first meeting to under an hour. Prepare some questions or conversation points you want to cover and that you think would make the meeting more enjoyable for them. The key is to let the conversation flow relationally. Be sure to thank them for their time; they're a busy professional, like you aspire to be.

In his book, *How to Win Friends and Influence People,* Dale Carnegie talks about how you can get influential people to meet with you. You have to disregard your insecurity and at the same time proceed with humility. He writes how you should show genuine interest in the person, remember their name, really listen to them, be sincere, and smile. In other words, you should approach the meeting as though you're trying to make a friend. That's something really anyone can do.

67

After meeting, you can decide whether or not you want to take it another step. Did the person reciprocate your relational demeanor? Did they offer too much unsolicited advice or talk down to you? Did they ask you questions and seem sincere? Did you leave the meeting feeling inspired, interested, and engaged? In other words, did you feel like a real connection was made? If not, let it go as an attempt and nothing more. Then redirect your efforts to someone else. You don't want to waste your time forcing something that won't be good for either one of you in the long-run. If the meeting went well, however, then you'll want to immediately put together a follow-up plan.

Unlike with dating, it's okay to appear ambitious with a prospective mentor. You want this person to know A) very clearly what you're looking for and B) that you're serious and wouldn't be wasting their time if they take you on as a mentee. As such, it's appropriate to follow up immediately, and to thank your prospective mentor for their time. You can do this via email or text - or a phone call if that's the communication method they prefer. At the end of the call or message, mention that you'd like to meet again, and if they agree, offer to get something on the calendar. Be prepared to suggest a couple of days and times (usually three or four is standard). Remember, you're both still vetting each other at this point, so you want it to feel relaxed and not contrived.

Now is perhaps the hardest step. You have to let the relationship evolve organically, like with any other friendship. You don't want to place too high of expectations on your mentor, or even on yourself. You may be tempted to jump right into calling it a mentorship, to give it a sense of status and importance, but in reality, it's a relationship like any other. It needs to evolve at a healthy pace for both of you and will need to be based on mutual respect and trust. Just give it time for it to grow as it will. It may get challenging at times, which is just as well. This is when your mentor likely feels comfortable enough to really begin to sculpt something about your habits or ways that will give you lasting results. You may be tempted to push back, which is a normal reflex. Remember, what you do in response to this is crucial to your growth; this is what you signed up for. Rise to the challenge and develop some resiliency. This is where the good stuff happens. Also note this is not a matter of right or wrong. You and your mentor can have differing opinions; it's how you communicate about them that matters.

It's important to take initiative in different ways to help guide the relationship. For instance, you can set a regular schedule, adapt to your mentor's preferred meeting times or places, and come to every meeting with talking points and questions you'd like to cover. This will make sure you're making the best use of your time. It will also be good for you to learn how to anticipate problems and to offer solutions (when appropriate) for your mentor as you would for anyone else you're close to. You want to understand their professional and personal priorities much the same way you'd like them to do with you. You can ask more from your mentor without demanding it; this won't bother them, quite the opposite. It will make them feel honored and appreciated for their expertise. Finding ways to solidify the bond you've created will only strengthen the relationship.

Be sure to periodically ask your mentor for feedback. This can be a difficult pill to swallow at times, but it's also good for you. This will be the number one way you grow over time and will be a highlight for both of you. Asking for feedback may initially feel weird, but eventually, it should become almost second-nature, and you'll find yourself thirsting for words you used to fear. A good mentor will also treat these times with great care and sensitivity. Keep in mind that this entire process will take your continued commitment to it. It's not like a summer internship; mentoring takes more time and energy. Only when you dedicate yourself to the process will you be able to understand what it means to be a student on the path to expertise.

Know the A-Listers in Your Niche

Similar to the research phase in finding a mentor, you want to, more broadly, understand who in your field is making waves. If you want to get spotted on the radar and learn the things that you should definitely know, then your best bet will be to learn from the professionals who are in that niche. It will be fairly easy to spot them because they're basically the most referenced or active people on the scene. If they're not, then you can easily Google keywords for your niche and look at the top-ranking blogs, articles, or book authors. Finding these professionals is just the beginning. Following and being recognized by them is the next step, and much more difficult.

You need to follow these people, first of all, because they matter (at least in your niche). Sure, you can ramble that you have ideas worth hearing all you want on various spaces throughout the internet, but if no one knows you, no one cares, and so it's all fairly pointless. Instead, you can follow these people and learn from their ways. How they do the things they do is the standard for your field. If you want to rise, you have to either meet their quality or surpass their skills. Of course, getting recognized by them is a bit tricky, because why do they need to recognize you? What do you offer them? Try and build something worthy as you create your own network. Decide where your value is and show it.

Their opinion matters, and so does their social circle. Simply lingering around their blogs won't be enough. You want to always remember to leave a mark. Comment, join anything that's happening online (such as a webinar or comment on videos or something similar), and better yet, correspond with notable authors or bloggers. Most likely they'll be too busy to answer, but at the very least you're trying by reaching out and creating an avenue of connection. You can help your case by making sensible, response-worthy messages to help get your replies. While more difficult than meeting in person, you can approach this in much the same relationship-building way as you would with a mentor. If your niche is one that has in-person events you'll also want to attend as many as possible. Meet-ups, conferences, happy hour groups, or any other kind of social networking events; make it a point to attend as many as you can. You can bet these are the places where the experts and A-Listers will be, which means you definitely want to be there as well.

This also means you should rigorously follow trends in your niche. Every field undergoes change, some more rapidly than others. Experts are those people who always stay at the forefront of what's happening. They explore new trends to understand where their industry is headed. This provides you with foresight as well as insight. While others are unaware of the shifting waves of progress, experts can more easily and quickly connect the dots so they can take advantage of the change that's coming. You can stay abreast of trends by setting up specific Google Alerts for trends you are following, or subscribe to blogs and websites like TrendHunter. Another big thing you can do is to commit to reading more. Look for and read industry analyst reports, as they try to predict industry trends over the next ten years. It doesn't hurt to ping your network if you see a new trend, to see what they think.

Define (& Re-Define) Your Network

Networking is an important part of enriching your personal and professional life. It could be the key to you landing your dream job. However, even the most extroverted people struggle with how to network in an effective way. The idea of making connections with strangers can be intimidating, and knowing where to start can be tough. Despite these challenges, sculpting a network that really does work for you will be invaluable as you dedicate yourself to learning something new and becoming a valued expert in the field.

Let's start by defining what it is. Your professional network is a group of people that have connected over a common theme that is relevant to your work. You are all coming together for business or career reasons, searching for avenues of professional connection. This could be a way for you to find out about job leads, but in reality, if done right, it is so much more than that. Besides being a place where you can solve work-related problems, find recommendations for vendors or suppliers, and be exposed to information about prospective employers, employees, and clients, your network is where you go to learn. Members of your network are who you go to with questions and concerns, and more broadly who you learn from. It's your learning community for you to bounce ideas off of and integrate within as you discover new information and deepen your existing knowledge about your field.

So who should be in your network? This unique group can be made up of almost anyone you've ever met, as long as they check a few boxes. You want these people to have a good character and to somehow bolster your goals. Start by looking in the obvious places: your previous and current workplaces. Current and former coworkers are people with whom you already have some point of connection, so it's an easy way to begin. Chances are they can introduce you to someone else who has similar interests or who may be a helpful contact as you grow in your field.

Additionally, you'll want to research and attend professional conferences and events where you can be exposed to and connect with like-minded people with similar career goals. See what kinds of

73

professional associations exist in your area that will introduce you to attendees of interest. Many conferences have a list of organizations or employers who are attending their upcoming conference, so, with some diligence, you can see who you may want to connect with beforehand. Before attending a conference, make sure you have updated business cards with your non-work contact information and bring them with you. If you especially enjoy the conference, and if it's an option, you may opt to become an active member of the association or organization that held it. You could serve on a committee or volunteer for the next conference. This will give your colleagues a chance to see you in action.

In addition to events and conferences, you can use your LinkedIn page and/or Facebook to make connections with others, although studies show in-person meeting is typically best for longer term connections. As a starting point, though, these can be helpful in getting your foot in the door with someone. Keep your LinkedIn page maintained, much the same way as you would your resume. Post about your accomplishments, newsworthy developments in your field, and make connections with others from your field, your school, or your favorite companies.

Keep in mind your friends and family are also valuable parts of your network. Talk to these people about your career goals and aspirations. Chances are they know someone through their own network that has some helpful information for you. You never know who will be able to give you guidance and support, so speak up! Doing so can also build bridges in your personal life as well, as it will help you get to know your extended or in-law family. In a similar vein, remember your former professors or instructors from college, graduate school, or even high school. If you were close with a teacher, or a memorable student in some way, keep in touch. These people can either connect you to other contacts or be mentors to you in some way. Former classmates can do the same. If your university has meet-ups or reunions, try to attend as many as possible, and to connect with other students who were in the same classes or graduated with a similar degree. As you get older, these contacts will continue to get more and more valuable. If you were a member of a fraternity or sorority, you can look here as well.

Volunteering for charity is another way you can network to meet people who are engaged in the community while also working towards social betterment. It's a great way to casually get to know others from a non-professional vantage point that may feel a bit more natural to some. You may even discover something you didn't know about yourself, or find a new skill or field you want to grow in. Plus, when you volunteer, you not only gain experience and exposure to other like-minded people, you make a difference for a group of people. Besides looking great on your resume or LinkedIn, you can feel good about the good you are doing.

It will be important as you define and redefine your network that you keep it alive and healthy. Don't treat it like a dusty old book on a shelf that you only access every year or so to reference one or two things. Think of it as an organism. It is a living, breathing thing that must be tended to or it will fade. The last thing you want is to reach out to someone who doesn't remember you or to miss out on a great opportunity because you have a contact who knows about it but doesn't think of you. You'll want to make plans to stay connected with people in your network. If you have people who aren't local to you, then make sure they know they have a standing invitation to meet up if they're ever in your city. Send a few key emails or notes to your core network every year so they know what you're up to. The holidays are an ideal time to do this, as are times when you're making a change such as starting a new job or moving to a new city.

As you continue to sculpt your network, keep in mind who you know is more important than how many people you know. This is where "quality over quantity" rings true! Jim Rohn, personal development guru, says that we're the average of the five people we spend the most time with. That can be a scary thought for some of us. Think about who those five people are for you. If you want to up your professional game, you will need to surround yourself with people who elevate and inspire you. The people around you have a huge impact on your life, so it is important for you to surround yourself with the right people. It is critical for you to find people who inspire you, who share a similar mindset with you, or who can act as mentors. You need people in your life who will push you rather than pull you in harmful directions that can hold you back.

Take a minute to consider who you spend the majority of your time with. Who are your closest five friends? How do you support them? How do they support you? Do they inspire you and challenge you to be better? How do you feel around them? Do they build you up? Do they in some way hold you back? The values that people you spend time with have will seep into your life and your values system, for better and for worse. That is why it is so important for you to be in alignment with people you are around. Otherwise, you will be dissatisfied or lose sight of your own goals and values. If you spend time with people who are motivated, hard-working, happy, successful, and healthy, then you will begin to experience some of those positive side effects yourself. You will feel inspired to grow and develop to match those traits so you better emulate them yourself. The more you emulate them, the more you attract them back into your life. It becomes a positive feedback of giving and receiving goodness and inspiration.

As you grow and prune your network, just remember to be genuine and keep an open mind. You never know who you could meet. Be bold and respectful. If you're attending an event with hiring managers, ask one for an informational interview. Reach out to professionals in your network and beyond. Most importantly, don't let your shyness stop you. Those who struggle with shyness are in danger of missing out on the benefits of professional networking. Keep in mind, everyone struggles with this; it is not easy to reach out to others. Start with resources like LinkedIn and Facebook, and gradually work towards reaching out for in-person meetups. You can also begin by looking for situations in which you feel the most comfortable and to then use those opportunities to form relationships. For example, when you participate in an activity you enjoy you will meet other people who also enjoy it. Likewise, doing volunteer work will give you the opportunity to meet people with whom you have something in common. Start small and build from there.

Never Stop Learning

This one is huge. You would think at some point experts would have learned everything they could learn to be where they are as experts. That's just not true; experts never stop learning. Ever! As a matter of fact, most people, once they become an expert, will actually commit to learning more. The reason for this is simple. Once you are an expert and begin to enjoy the benefits of being an expert, you will want to stay an expert. Beyond being proud of this accomplishment, experts have the drive to stay knowledgeable and to be informed. Typically, experts read more, continue to educate themselves through courses and workshops, regularly gather knowledge from other experts, and are constantly looking for new ways to learn and grow.

Experts tend to want to digest new information on different topics as often as they can. They never want to stop learning. As you commit yourself to develop into an expert, you will want to visit new blogs every now and again, and to try something new. Doing so will help you think beyond the box. If you are still interested in learning, why not go beyond your niche and invest time in understanding another, related niche? Try designing, or internet marketing, or coding. The options are endless! I've grown so much from trying new things. You have no idea how powerful it is to integrate SEO, blogging, and internet marketing together until you try it and see the results. Learning new things like this can (literally and figuratively) open yourself up to a lot of opportunities.

There's nothing better that can improve your existing skillset, and overall make you more competitive, than combining several multi-disciplines into one mind. The results are incredible. It will be such a breakthrough for you, both personally and professionally. It is the key to your success.

The more you learn, the more people will want to listen to what you have to say. You may even find yourself becoming a thought leader in your field. Experts are never content with what is, or the status quo. As a rule, they're always looking for the next step or evolution of their profession. They are constantly trying new techniques, improving on existing concepts, exploring new ideas, and adding value wherever and however they can. They strive to push the boundaries and expand the limits of their field. Experts devote themselves to leading the way for the future of their profession with true vision. To get to this point, you'll have to start small with a big vision. Perhaps you can begin a blog or do very specific updates on your social media channels around your area of expertise. Or you could consider writing a simple ebook, submit a white paper to a professional organization, or write articles for online publications. Keep in mind that becoming a thought leader is not a sprint; it's a marathon. You get there by doing lots of little things well.

As you grow in your learning, you also want to be sure to share your knowledge with others. Experts become more valuable by sharing their skills and knowledge with people around them who could benefit from it. They always want to be of service to their professional community. If you want to be seen as an expert, put your expertise out there for all

79

to benefit from, and do not be afraid of being judged. Try to let go of your fears, and put your thoughts and ideas (based on your expertise) out there. One way you can share your knowledge is to train others, say by speaking at a small event or industry conference in your local city. Remember as you seek these opportunities out that it's not about you. Consider your audience and the ways in which getting your message out there will improve the field. You have to be seen as someone who confidently shares information and expects nothing (within reason) in return. Sharing your knowledge also helps you absorb the information better to help you further your study.

Chapter Summary

To move from a basic level into expertise, you will have to prioritize a few key actions - and stick with them! These are: finding a mentor in your field with whom you can form a quality relationship and who challenges you in productive ways; knowing the A-listers in your field who are at the forefront of what's happening and understand where your industry is headed; sculpting a network that really works for you and your pursuit to becoming a valued expert in the field; and digesting plenty of new information on different topics as often as you can - so you never stop learning. In the next chapter, you'll learn actions you can take to improve your memory that will help you along your learning path.

CHAPTER EIGHT

IMPROVING YOUR MEMORY

In many ways, memories shape who we are because they make up our internal realities. They are stories of ourselves, and they are the stories of what we are capable of learning through our ability to recall necessary information at relevant times. There are several factors that have been tied to reasons for improved (or easily degraded) memory - anything from genes to nutrition to meditation practices. In general, reducing your sugar intake, avoiding high caloric foods, and getting plenty of exercise is highly recommended in order to have better memory function.

Living both a physically and mentally active life will be important overall in your ability to retain your brain function longer because, just as the rest of your muscles grow stronger with use, so too do mental exercises help maintain mental skills and memory. Exercise is tied to stress reduction and improved positivity, which are both crucial to prioritize as you commit to learning something new. Some sources even call for an increase in caffeine to help boost memory (and performance) even if only in short-term contexts (such as during a study session, or for a test or a big presentation). Beyond that, the core practices below will help you improve your memory as you learn a new skill.

Sleep More (& Better)

Many people find themselves cutting back on sleep the busier they get, even though they recognize how important sleep is for their overall health. It can be tempting to convince yourself that sleeping isn't productive and that sacrificing a good night's sleep before an important presentation, exam, or workday will yield positive results. We tend to think of sleep as a luxury versus a necessity; however, when it comes to learning and memory, sleeping is actually one of the most important things you can do.

Research has found that people who suffer from sleep disorders often have impaired memory functions. Cognitive scientists at Washington University have found evidence that people who sleep after processing and storing a memory carry out their intentions much better than people who try to execute their plan before getting some sleep. This gives new meaning to the phrase 'sleep on it!' Researchers have shown that sleep enhances our ability to remember to do something in the future, something referred to as prospective memory. Our ability to carry out the future actions we intend is not so much based on how those intentions are embedded in our memories, but rather a trigger we encounter later on by some particular context that sparks our recall of those intentions. Prospective memory, or things we intend to do, include such things as remembering to take a pill, remembering to buy our friend a gift, or bringing home the right groceries from the store. We use this form of memory every single day. Researchers believe the prospective memory process occurs during something called slow wave sleep, an

82

early pattern in the sleep cycle that is very conducive to memory strengthening. These findings convey the importance of making sure you get to sleep after making plans or to-do lists before you execute the plan itself. In short, sleep helps us strengthen our associations between the task that we intend to do and the context that triggers the memory of this task.

Sleep also helps with memory consolidation and improves our ability to remember what we learned during the day. Deep sleep, or non-REM sleep, can strengthen memories if the sleep occurs within twelve hours of the initial learning. This has important implications for how you time your study and sleep schedule. If your current schedule doesn't allow you to get the recommended seven to eight hours of sleep every night, then you can prioritize sleep on the weekends. Research has found sleep deprivation to be detrimental to attention span, alertness, and reaction times, which are clearly things that you need in order to have a productive workday. What's good is that getting just one full night of sleep will restore your cognitive functioning back to normal. These recovery periods are not the ideal replacement for getting good sleep consistently throughout the weeks, but they do work as long as they are fairly regular - for example, every weekend for at least nine or ten hours.

Studies have also shown how memories that are associated with a reward are also reinforced by sleep. Sleep helps strengthen memories, and it also helps you choose and retain the memories that have a rewarding value because rewards act as a mental tag that works to seal information into your mind as you learn it. During periods of sleep, the information is solidified, which means taking a short nap as you learn can help you cement new facts and skills in your memory. In other words, taking a nap after a period of learning is beneficial for your long-term retention.

Try Mnemonic Devices

Memory can be broken down into sensory memory, short-term memory, and long-term memory. Sensory memory is when our senses help us to receive and record and recall information. Short-term memory is when we remember what we have recently seen or heard. For instance, you may recall a phone number you just looked up or the name of a person you just met. Long-term memory, in contrast, is when you transfer short-term memories into your deeper, more lasting memory that has no capacity on the amount of storage. Information gets into long-term memory through repetition or visualizing information so you can recall the information later, much like a filing cabinet. We often need cues to help trigger us to recall information from our long-term memories. That is where mnemonics come into play.

Mnemonics are techniques we can use to help us improve our ability to remember something. They are memory devices that help your brain better absorb and recall important information. Mnemonics are simple shortcuts that allow us to associate the information we want to remember with an image, a sentence, or a word. Think of mnemonics as ways to give your brain a boost with tasks it can do anyway. Often, the information you want is in your brain somewhere, and all you need is a tool to help you reach it more quickly when it counts. As we age we'll experience a decrease in memory function. This results in slower thinking, decreased concentration, slower memory processing, and a higher need for more memory cues. In these instances, mnemonics can also be used to help keep memory sharp. In any case, these memory techniques make it easier for us to remember facts and can be applied to nearly any subject.

Mnemonics will help you simplify, summarize, and compress information to make it easier to learn. It can be especially handy for students in medical school or law school, or people studying a foreign language. Basically, if you need to memorize and store large amounts of new information, you can try a mnemonic and you'll find that you remember the information long after you pass your test. The following is a list of the most popular mnemonic devices you can use.

The Method of Loci

Loci is the plural of 'locus,' which also means location, and in Ancient Greece, they used this mnemonic device for easy memorization. The method of loci involves the mental strategy of imagining yourself in a room you are familiar with, and then taking note of items around the room, such as the couch, lamp, piano bench, photo album, and so on. You then pair the items that you mentally place in the room with the pieces of information that you are trying to learn, such as a list of things that you need to remember in a certain order. You can visualize yourself walking back through that room and then picking up or passing by each item that you placed there, thus triggering your recall for that information. The method of loci has been proven to be a very effective method for learning. Research has demonstrated how it leads to a significant improvement in the ability to recall information in multiple cases, from college students to adult learners. Some research has also suggested that using mnemonic techniques such as the method of loci is effective in improving the ability to learn and remember information for people with mild forms of cognitive impairment. This is likely because the method of loci uses elaborative rehearsal, which involves manipulating information by adding meaning to it and using it, rather than only studying a list and repeating it.

Acronyms & Acrostics

Acronyms are typically the most familiar type of mnemonic strategies, ones you're most likely fairly familiar with. They use a simple formula of a letter to represent each word or phrase that needs to be remembered. Think of the NBA, which stands for the National Basketball Association. While an acronym is a word formed from the first letters or groups of letters in a name or phrase, an acrostic is a series of lines from which certain letters (such as the first letters of all lines) form a word or phrase. These can then be used as mnemonic devices by taking the first letters of words or names that need to be remembered and developing an acronym or acrostic. Take music class for instance. If you have to remember the order of notes so you can identify and play the correct one while reading music, you can remember the notes of the treble staff as EGBDF. The most common acrostic used for learning this is *Every Good Boy Does Fine*. The notes on the bass staff are ACEG, which is most commonly translated into the acrostic *All Cows Eat*

Grass. An often-used acrostic in math class is *Please Excuse My Dear Aunt Sally*, which represents the order of operations in algebra and stands for parentheses, exponents, multiplication, division, addition, and subtraction.

Rhymes & Music

Rhyming words can be used as a mnemonic to help us learn and recall information. A rhyme is a saying that has a similar terminal sound at the end of each line. Rhymes are easier to remember because they can be stored by acoustic encoding in our brains. For example, *In fourteen hundred and ninety-two Columbus sailed the ocean blue.* The ability to memorize and remember these kinds of phrases is often due in part to repetition and in part to rhyming. Think of nursery rhymes you were brought up singing. You can rearrange words or substitute a different word with the same meaning to make them rhyme. Think of the familiar spelling rule, *i before e, except after c.* This phrase sticks in our memories because we've heard it multiple times (repetition), and also because of the rhyming within it. You can also use music to encode the information into your brain. Remember the ABC song you learned as a kid? Music has been proven to stick with us long-term, so search online and find there are plenty of songs that exist to help you learn certain information - anything from state capitals to the countries in Africa, and beyond!

Chunking & Organizing

Chunking information is a mnemonic strategy that works by organizing information into more easily learned groups, phrases, words or numbers. More simply, it is a way of breaking down larger pieces of information into smaller, organized chunks that are easier to manage. In the United States, our telephone numbers do this for us, so we can more easily recall them. If you have to memorize a long digit phone number, 123456789101112 (and it wasn't so easy to do because it's in order), it would likely take some effort to remember. However, if you break it down into more digestible pieces, such as 12345 6789 101112, it will be easier to recall. Chucking has also been studied as a means of helping those with early stages of Alzheimer's disease improve their verbal working memory.

In a similar vein, organizing information into either objective or subjective categories helps with memorization. Objective organization means you place information into well-recognized, logical categories. For example, trees and grass are plants, and a cricket is an insect. Subjective organization, on the other hand, is when you categorize what appears to be unrelated items in a way that helps you recall the items later by ascribing meaning to them, such as trees, grass, and crickets being things you might find in a meadow. This can be useful because it breaks down the amount of information to learn. If you can divide a list of items into a fewer number of categories, then all you have to remember is the categories that will then serve as memory cues in the future. An example of this is relating to how you ride a bike with learning how to drive a car.

Keywords

If you're studying a second - or even third or fourth - language, then using the keyword mnemonic method will significantly improve your learning and recall. A keyword mnemonic is an elaborative rehearsal strategy that helps encode information more effectively because it ascribes meaning to the content you're trying to memorize. A keyword mnemonic involves two steps. You first have to choose a keyword that sounds somewhat similar to the word you're trying to learn, and then you form a mental image of that keyword as being somehow connected to the new piece of information. Studies have shown that visualization and association trigger the recall of the correct word. Let's say you're learning French, and you want to memorize the word *parler*, which means to speak. Every time you think of this word, you associate it with a pearl coming out of your mouth. By visualizing it this way, when you see *parler*, you will think of the pearl in your mouth and recall what *parler* means in French.

Linking & Connecting

The linking method for mnemonics consists of developing a story or image that connects pieces of information together that you need to remember. Each item leads you to recall the next item. For instance, you know you need to bring your glasses, keys, notebook, lunch, and wallet with you to work every day, so you can think of a short story to help you remember everything. Jill's notebook needs special keys so it can open her glasses, which she needs to see her hungry wallet that holds her lunch. If you add humor to the story, it's even easier for you to recall this kind of information. A similar strategy involves making meaningful connections with something that you are already familiar with or know. Making this kind of connection is another kind of elaborative rehearsal, which I've mentioned above. An example of this is if you meet a man named Ned and you notice he is unusually friendly. To help you remember his name, you can think of him as Neighbor Ned or Neighborly Ned so that the next time you see him, you can more easily recall his name.

The more you can relate new concepts to ideas that you already understand, the faster you'll learn the new information. Memory plays a central role in our ability to carry out complex cognitive tasks, such as applying knowledge to problems we haven't encountered before and drawing inferences from facts we already know. By finding ways to fit new information with pre-existing knowledge, you'll find additional layers of meaning in the new material. This will help you fundamentally understand it better, and you'll be able to recall it more accurately. When you connect the new to the old, you give yourself mental hooks on which to hang new knowledge.

However, you go about using mnemonics to help you improve your memory, keep in mind that you want to incorporate imagination, association, and location. If you create images that are engaging and vivid, you will be more likely to recall that information. Likewise, your brain wants to link ideas; it's constantly looking for ways to associate pieces of information, so if you can, link concepts together as a means of remembering new information. Location is also a great way to integrate new material into your memory because you already have so much knowledge about the places you know.

You also want to remember the learning techniques I discussed from earlier chapters that will help speed up your learning as well as retain it for longer. Remember how images activate our learning so much more than information that is verbal or written? We are great at recognizing visuals and can easily invent our own to help guide our memories. If you need to remember a task that you have to do in the future, try creating a vivid mental image of it actually happening. When you meet someone new, spend a few seconds picturing something about them that might give you a visual reminder of their name. Whatever the case, ascribing images and meaning will be invaluable to you for your recall. Using mnemonic memory strategies can give you that boost in your memory that we all need, and it can likewise improve your efficiency in learning. Keep in mind that you may need to practice a few of these strategies before they come easily, but once you have them down, they should stay with you long-term.

Create Memory Palaces

A memory palace is taking the method of loci to a new level. This mnemonic is when you think of an imaginary location in your mind where you can store specific, meaningful images. The most common type of memory palace is when you make a journey or path through a place you know well, like a building, town, or route. Along that path, there are specific locations that you are used to always visiting that are also in the same order. Think of your memory palace as a place that you can easily visualize where you store new or important information. You will associate a memory journey or path with an actual journey or path.

You first want to choose a place you know very well, like your home or place of work. Reacquaint yourself with this place as needed. You may need to walk around it several times, take pictures, and so on, so you feel like you really know it. Try to visualize the entire place. It doesn't have to be in incredible detail, all you need to be able to do is to orient yourself and move around the space in your mind. Visit the place as often as you need to in order to do this mentally. Once you have, you can begin to plan or map your route. It should have a starting point and an endpoint. For example: the bottom of the stairs, the top of the stairs, the closet, the hallway, shoes outside your bedroom door, bathroom, shower, and so on, until you find a logical endpoint. You will be able to revise your memory palace after you test it a few times, so don't worry if it's not perfect your first go at it. If you have a lot to learn, you will make many different memory palaces.

You'll next want to find a different place where you can relax and really visualize the place you chose for your route. Practice following your route a few times, first forwards, and then backward. Remember, you can always make changes to it if you find there are hiccups anywhere. When you have your route down, then you want to assign certain stations (or loci) where you will store new information in. Each locus should be unique and serve as a separate image that you don't want to confuse with other stations along your route. Go back along your route and make sure the places you have picked are unique. Again, practice doing this forwards and backwards, so you really know your route.

Now that you have your memory palace and route primed, and your stations selected, you want to begin to assign new learning to it. Take a list of something you want to memorize, like a shopping list or key vocabulary words you want to learn. Take one or two items at a time and place a mental image of them in each locus of your memory palace. Try doing a few at a time and practicing as you go, so you can really begin to associate your list with your route. You also may want to try exaggerating the images of the items to have them really interact with the location. For example, if the first item on your list to memorize is an apple, and the first locus in your memory palace is the front door, picture a giant apple walking through your front door. Because we are such visual learners, making your mnemonic images come alive with your senses will improve your ability to remember them. Exaggeration of the images and humor will always help you recall them in the future. Keep in mind that you can also use spaced repetition to get this information into your long-term memory. Spaced repetition, also called the distributed study practice (which I discussed earlier on in this book) is a learning technique you can use that incorporates increasing intervals of time between when you review new material, so you can strengthen your recall ability.

A solid memory palace strategy is, without a doubt, the most effective way to study efficiently. Their use has been recorded in history for over a thousand years, and they have even, most likely, been used back during the hunter-gatherer times. Memory palaces are used by mental athletes during memory competitions (where people perform feats like memorizing a shuffled deck of cards and so on in only a few minutes), as well as for schoolwork and learning - even for memorizing an entire book. As a memory technique, it unlocks your spatial memory and spatial mapping. The more you create and use memory palaces, the more they unlock multiple levels and layers of memory that you can use in order to learn faster. These levels of memory include: autobiographical memory, episodic memory, semantic memory, procedural memory, figurative memory, and more. Each of these is unlocked through this memorization strategy that is devoted to improving your memory as you study. It will make your study sessions so much faster and more powerful.

Chapter Summary

Improving your memory begins with the most important element in learning a new skill: sleep. Sleep aids memory consolidation and improves our ability to remember what we learned during the day. It can strengthen our memories and is irreplaceable as a learning tool. If your current schedule doesn't allow you to get the recommended seven to eight hours of sleep every night, find a time when you can prioritize sleep. It's that important! Mnemonics are simple shortcuts that allow us to associate the information we want to remember with an image, a sentence, or a word. A memory palace is a specific kind of mnemonic device when you think of an imaginary location in your mind where you store specific, meaningful images to help you remember complex concepts. Both are memory tools you can use to help improve your memory. In the next chapter, I'll overview what you can do if you find yourself needing to cram.

CHAPTER NINE

HOW TO CRAM (WHEN YOU HAVE TO)

Let's face it, we only pull all-nighters when we've fallen behind. Cognitive scientists have conducted study after study that demonstrates that cramming doesn't help us as long-term learners. Attempting to cram all of this new information into our brains uses (and over-uses) our short-term memory. Remember that with long-term learning what we need is our long-term memory to help us recall and retain most facts.

Short-term memory tends to fade rapidly, so if we don't reuse that information quickly, it will disappear within a period of a few minutes to a few hours. Cramming, in general, doesn't allow this new information to move from short-term to long-term memory, which is critical for performing well over time. Remember, the best study method is breaking it down in intervals, and it's always better to begin early - both early on in your learning and early on in the day. Studies show our body clocks tend to prepare us to perform better during the day and in the morning as opposed to later on in the day. Early in the morning studying is typically more recommended than late at night studying.

In this day and age, we will all encounter sleep deprivation at some point in our lives, whether willingly or unwillingly. There are the days when the responsibilities seem endless. Studies have shown that staying awake all night is not beneficial to your study habits. You will actually work better the next day if you have a good night's rest. Our brains lose their efficiency with sleep deprivation, so instead of staying up all night and missing out on the recommended amount of sleep (experts suggest anywhere between seven to nine hours), it's much better to rest your brain and wake up early for a last-minute study session. Cramming, in general, makes us feel overwhelmed, frustrated, and keeps us asking questions we cannot typically answer under pressure. Where do you start? How do you begin? It will make you feel more overwhelmed than you need to feel, so try to avoid it.

All the same, we all find ourselves from time to time in a situation where we are trying to quickly catch up on information or a project - and time is running out. If the unthinkable happens, and you find yourself the night before an exam or a big presentation, faced with the prospect of having to pull an all-nighter, there are a few things you can still do to give yourself a higher chance of performing well.

To begin with, don't panic. If you are in a high-stress state of mind, your concentration will be shot, try to relax first and foremost. If it helps, try something like meditation or a short walk before beginning your cram session. Once you're in a good mental place, make sure you have all your notes and books with you. You'll only need your books to look something up - in general, you'll want to use your notes to stick to the core things you'll need to remember. Have your pencil or pen, a notebook or legal pad, and some colored highlighters nearby in case you need them. Most importantly, turn off your social media. This form of addiction will only serve to distract you and make your cram session ineffective. Take a break from Facebook, silence your phone, turn off the TV, and get ready to focus. You're going to need all of your energy directed towards the content you're trying to learn last minute.

Now work on breaking your study material down into more digestible pieces. If you have an exam coming up solely based on one book and you procrastinated all semester and didn't do the assigned readings, focus on what you really need to know. Look at the chapters and remember three things per chapter. Essentially what you're doing is focusing on the big ideas and key details. Because you're officially cramming now, your learning has a shelf life. You want to stick to the basics and parse out the main ideas because those are the most likely points to be on the test. You have limited energy, so you want to direct it to key headings, dates, chargers, passages, vocabulary, themes, motifs, and so on. Filter out all the rest.

You can use a study guide as the foundation for your cramming - and even better, if you don't have one, you can make one. This will help you filter the materials you have into information you can focus on. It doesn't have to be neat, or perfect. Write it out, read it out loud, and revise it where it makes sense to. You can even ask a peer to give you feedback on it, or use it as a guide for a study group. Teaching the material to others will help you retain the information better.

Cramming is about finding a good rhythm, so if it helps, set a timer to break it up into sections. Using a timer will help you find a good study rhythm. If you study for eight hours straight, you're more likely to fall asleep during your test than you are to ace it. I recommend a five to one split. For every five parts of study, give yourself one part of anything else. For example, if you study for fifty minutes, then take a ten-minute break to play soccer, listen to music, take a snack break, or something similar. Your choice, just give yourself a nice break - and then get back to it.

If you've ever worried that all the information you've crammed in during a study session might not stay in your memory, research suggests a quick bout of exercise may actually help solidify some of it. One study found that when students did moderate exercise - such as running - after a period of learning (including cramming for an exam), they actually performed better than if they only crammed.

The active nature of exercise helps the brain retain new information and recall it when desired, whereas a passive activity, such as playing a computer game, does not. The stress hormone, cortisol, is known to have an impact on our memory retention. In some circumstances, cortisol can help us remember things, and in others, it impairs our memory. There are two types of stress in this sense, psychological and physical. Researchers think chemicals are released by physical activity, like running, which then improves memory retention. Researchers also recommend talking out loud as you cram, so you involve your auditory memory as you re-learn (or just learn) salient content. Make hand motions, use funny voices, pace around your apartment - do whatever it takes to keep yourself in an active learning state.

As you cram for your exam, presentation, or whatever it is you are cramming for, you will want to set an end time to it so you have the motivation to finish, and also so you can prioritize sleep at some point. If you need extra motivation, give yourself a reward at the end of this stretch too. Maybe it's your favorite sushi dinner, or ice cream, or chocolate, or a glass of wine. The key is you can't have it until you're done studying. Deadlines and rewards will help you stay on track. If you're a dedicated dieter, use carrots and hummus instead. Whatever you need to do, set some kind of personal goal for yourself that will help you keep moving forward without stagnating or getting bogged down.

Chapter Summary

Cramming makes us feel overwhelmed and frustrated, and is generally not recommended. There are a few things you can do if you find yourself in this position, however, and it involves breaking your study material down into more digestible pieces. Focus only on what you really need to know. Look at key chapters, headings, or notes, and remember the main ideas and critical details. Stick with the basics. Exercise will also help your brain retain this new information and recall it more easily, so take a run in between cram sessions. Lastly, and most importantly - prioritize sleep. It is the single best thing you can do for your performance. In the final chapter, I will give you pointers on how you can train your brain to stay focused.

CHAPTER TEN

TRAIN YOUR BRAIN TO STAY FOCUSED

If you're like me, you find yourself having days when you feel like everything is happening all at once. It's like you can't think straight, or even begin to make a plan because everything is coming at you constantly. The to-do list never seems to end. During such times, it's even more important for you to get organized and to slow down. Prioritizing this above your to-do list will help you get on track and in the long-run will actually help you work through things more quickly. Productive people will often spend a few minutes every morning organizing their day. They look at their calendars, make a prioritization list, set reminders for themselves throughout the day, and so on. In many cases, more productive people will also boost their productivity by resisting the temptation to be constantly accessible to others. So how can you be more like productive people? I have three key recommendations that I detail below that will help you train your brain to stay focused.

Beware of Digital Distractions

In today's world, we are increasingly bombarded with distractions to our work. Studies have shown that it can take more than twenty minutes to fully return our attention to an interrupted task. Constant phone calls, incoming emails, and colleagues stopping for a chat or with a "quick" question can seriously disrupt our train of thought and workflow. More productive people will set aside specific times for answering emails or returning calls and texts in order to build efficiency. It may take some adjustment for colleagues or clients, but with good communication these schedules are possible.

The internet itself has provided learners with a range of helpful search tools that give us so many positives in terms of learning and research; however, studies indicate teachers are concerned these kinds of technologies are creating more easily distracted generations of learners who have shorter attention spans. Some even think they distract more than they help students academically - that the negative outweighs the positive. Too many students today, "research" and "Google" are synonymous words. To these students, the process of doing research has shifted from a relatively slow method of intellectual curiosity and discovery to a much more fast-paced, short-term exercise with the end goal of locating just enough information to complete an assignment. Some teachers reported that, specifically, they are concerned their students will become over-dependent on search engines and will struggle with how to determine the quality of sources they discover, which will affect literacy rates as well as have lasting consequences on attention span, time management development, and critical thinking capacity. Many teachers also reported that, despite their students being raised in such a digital age, they are surprisingly lacking in their online search skills, such as having patience and determination in looking for information that is hard to find.

The repercussions of relying on digital learning are more critical for younger learners than adult learners, and yet are still important to note. Regardless of your age, overexposure to technology can result in a lack of focus and diminished ability to retain knowledge. For adult learners, these findings should primarily serve as a caveat to not get sucked into the digital realm too much when trying to learn something new. Because the internet and related technologies are so immediate, they work against our attentional control. Attentional control is our source of attention in our minds. It helps us maintain awareness (or alertness), process and orient information from sensory input, and resolve inconsistencies or conflicts in our learning. The effects of anxiety on attentional control are key to understanding the relationship between anxiety and performance. In general, studies have found anxiety inhibits our attentional control on a specific task by impairing our processing efficiency. Digital distractions work in much the same way.

If you're wondering what this has to do with your learning, the answer is: everything. How your brain can stay focused and on task ultimately determines how well you will learn something new. Only when you are able to fully concentrate will you be able to dedicate yourself to your learning endeavor. You will find that you can retain information much more easily when your brain isn't being constantly distracted. Having a clear head will make such a difference. You will have to come to see the blocks of time you set aside for learning as

105

sacred to everything else (minus, of course, emergencies). You will want to set aside time in your day at some point where you can devote yourself purely to directing your focus to your learning. You have to really make yourself follow through on this because we tend to give in easily to distractions.

It can be tough to know where to begin when you sit down to learn. Something I've grown to be quite fond of is - depending on what the learning is, of course - pre-reading. I find that it's a great way to introduce your brain to new learning, get interested in the topic, and prime your brain for the learning ahead. Pre-reading is the process of skimming a text to find key ideas before you carefully read a text or a chapter of a text from start to finish. It's also called previewing or surveying, but either way, it's the same idea. It's a kind of inspectional reading where you can use certain clues like the table of contents or chapter headings as a roadmap for your learning. It will give you an overview that will increase your reading speed and efficiency. In general, you'll want to play an active part in your reading to help with your retention. Think as you read and pre-read. Look at titles, subtitles, chapter beginnings, introductions, chapter summaries, headings, study questions, and conclusions. You may even want to check the index if the book has one to see what range of topics will be covered, or read the publisher's blurb.

Pre-reading will help you see the big picture and the overall purpose for the reading ahead so you can direct your attention to the concepts that really matter. It will actually increase your capacity to understand the material you are studying. In many cases, taking only a few minutes to pre-read can help you with your overall comprehension and retention. Just think: if you build your understanding of the big picture before you even begin to read the text, you have a conceptual framework already in place. When you encounter a new detail or piece of evidence in your reading, your mind will know better what to do with it and how to organize it.

Ask yourself as you're pre-reading: what kind of clues is the text giving me for my future learning? How can I apply what I already know to what I'm going to be learning here? What is the author's purpose for telling me this? Generating these kinds of questions as you go will help you both identify and achieve your purpose in your learning. If for some reason you're short on time - say, if you're cramming for an upcoming exam or quiz - then you can prioritize the first and last paragraph of every chapter (or only the introduction and conclusion or chapter summaries), while keeping in mind each chapter heading. This method shouldn't be a substitute for actually reading the material (which you should do at a later point), but it will help give you a quick overview of the salient themes and concepts from the text. If you want to take pre-reading one step further, you can email yourself your pre-reading study guide and compare it to your notes once you've actually read the text. Emailing as a practice actually helps train your attention better, because for every non-topic related email you have in your inbox, you can help remind your brain of your earlier learning by periodically emailing yourself summaries of your notes. Just the act of doing more with the information will be helpful because you will be able to read back over it with fresh eyes.

Different people learn in different ways. For example, some people can learn and retain information better if they listen to background music or some kind of neutral noise. Even the general hustle and bustle of a coffee shop conversation or a busy shopping area can help some people direct their focus to their study. Other people prefer absolute stillness and silence. For either category of learner, headphones can be useful as a means to either provide sound or to cancel it and other distractions out. This is something you need to work out for yourself, where you fall on this spectrum. In terms of listening to music while you study, research suggests it depends on the content of the study. Music (mostly classical music) has been shown to provide mental boosts for clarity and focus when playing low in the background, specifically for tasks that don't require a lot of digesting of complex material. Tasks that require you to keep track of several pieces of information at one time while processing them as well place heavy demands on your working memory, and so may hinder your learning. Regardless, positive effects of background music have been found and it may certainly be worth trying out if you're struggling with focus.

Another key discovery by cognitive scientists is the importance of drinking water as you learn. Staying adequately hydrated has a number of other benefits: it's good for our skin and immune system, and it keeps our bodies functioning at optimum levels. Interestingly, staying hydrated is also critical for enhancing our cognitive abilities, and can actually make us smarter. One key study indicated that students who took (and drank) water with them into an examination room performed better than students who did not. Dehydration, on the other hand, can seriously affect how our brains are able to function. When you fail to drink water, you are basically making your brain work harder than usual to do the same tasks.

Use the Pomodoro Technique

I discussed the Pomodoro Technique in an earlier chapter, but in the context of information overload and concentration it takes on a new, improved meaning. Learners can use the Pomodoro Technique to help themselves focus throughout the workday and over time. This process involves taking timed breaks and having timed work sessions when working on a task so you can more easily restore your focus and reach your work goals. It will also help you avoid becoming overwhelmed or distracted in your learning. Especially if you are stressed or anxious, your brain will not be able to effectively store and process new information. The best way to prevent this kind of brain fatigue from happening to you during your learning is to give your brain a break in between using it for a specific learning or work task. This brain break is a state of rest, or redirecting your attention and shift to a new activity for a short time. Even a five-minute break can relieve brain fatigue so you are able to give your full attention back to your learning when you return to it.

People in several fields have used this technique in order to improve their productivity and concentration. Using the Pomodoro Technique will enable you to really stick with a task because it gives you both accountability and control over your work schedule in a way that organizes and motivates you. It will help you achieve better results in less overall time. How it works is you break your work into twenty-five-minute work sessions throughout the day. During these twenty-five minutes, you concentrate deeply on that particular task with as little distraction as possible. Then, you switch to something else during a quick break (usually around five minutes). You can repeat this as many times as you need throughout a workday. It may be best if you start with trying one or two of these sessions a day before trying to build up to three, four, or even five. I'd also recommend you start with a lower time slot (twenty-five minutes) before trying to work up to longer time slots (thirty-five or even forty-five minutes if you want to try it).

For your break, you can stand, walk around, have a snack, or scan an article in the news before you return your focus back to concentrating on your work. It's best if you keep these breaks to under ten minutes. Experts highly recommended you move around if you can during this break. Studies have shown how sitting (or even standing) for long periods of time can lead to increased risk for a number of health problems, including diabetes, heart disease, stroke, and decreases in brain function. In general, it's best for you to alternate sitting and standing at various points throughout the day, so you're not doing too much of either one. You can use your five minutes to stretch, grab a cup of coffee, or go on a quick walk outside around the building. Your brain will thank you for this!

If you're finding it difficult to begin a big task because you know it will take a long time, you're not alone. Most people do. What the Pomodoro Technique does for you, is it gets you to break this task down into blocks of work so that it's easier for you to digest over time. It can be tailored to your specific learning needs, so if you'd like, you can set a shorter time period for work, to help you gradually build up to the task. Likewise, you can make your breaks a little longer if you find that helps activate your work sessions better. On the official website, it's also recommended that learners try to estimate how many work periods are necessary to complete a particular project so you can better break it down by month, week, day, and perhaps even by a work session. This will inevitably help motivate you in reaching the finish line. Remember to block off your calendar and turn off your phone notifications to limit distractions so you can maintain your focus.

Try Meditation

Meditation is a simple practice that anyone can learn, at no cost, with no fancy equipment, and with no extensive training. It has been practiced for thousands of years by all kinds of people. One of the most common reasons people try meditation is to reduce stress and anxiety. Studies have shown meditation reduces levels of the stress hormone, cortisol. When we encounter something stressful, our cortisol levels increase. This was likely an adaptive reaction developed by our ancestors as a means of increasing their chances of survival during uncertain times. These days, our cortisol levels are influenced by other forms of mental stress that can have adverse physical effects on us, such as disrupting sleep, causing depression and anxiety, increasing blood pressure, and contributing to fatigue and demotivation. Research has shown over and over that meditation relieves these symptoms of stress and can even relieve a variety of other stress-related conditions, such as irritable bowel syndrome or post-traumatic stress disorder. Meditation can also reduce symptoms of anxiety disorders and anxiety-related mental health issues including panic attacks, obsessive or compulsive behaviors, and phobias. In turn, over time meditation will also help improve sleep patterns and reduce instances of insomnia, which is stress-induced as well. A related effect is reduced blood pressure, which decreases not only during the meditation practice, but also gradually in individuals who consistently meditate. Regular meditation can then reduce strain on the heart and arteries, which helps prevent heart disease.

The distractions our world presents to us make mindfulness activities like meditation critical to our ability to focus and stay focused on tasks. Some of these tools are essential for our work and social lives, so finding a balance in their usage is difficult yet necessary. Our ability to concentrate on tasks well determines our ability to create complete memories. Remember short-term and long-term memory? Complete memories are the product of deep and mindful learning. Our lack of attention to detail, or our tendency to want to rush through our learning, makes it difficult for us to remember crucial and important pieces of information. Having excellent concentration may not necessarily lead to better memory, but it is, however, essential to building a well-formed and useful ability to retain and recall information.

Unfortunately, there are more barriers to our concentration now than ever. The notification-saturated world of the internet constantly bombards our focus with bits of information that vary in their usefulness to us. You have to take an active role in creating that balance so you have an ideal work environment and so you achieve your goals. It's hard, too, because even merely thinking about your email or social media accounts will interrupt your concentration, so only going offline may be insufficient for your ability to focus.

If any of this sounds familiar to you, meditation could be the answer. Meditation has been found to help with increasing the strength and endurance of attention, memory retention, and problem-solving. Research has found consistent meditation practices can help people both reorient and maintain their attention for longer. This can help with creativity in solving problems as well as better task management and focus. Meditation has also been known to improve tendencies in mind-wandering, excessive or uncontrollable worry, and inability to stay focused or alert. Besides improvements in attention and clarity of thinking, meditation may also help keep your mind young and memory intact by reducing the chances of age-related memory loss. Some studies have even indicated the possibility of meditation to reverse or partially improve the effects of dementia. It is still relatively unclear to scientists the precise reason why meditation has the effects it does; however, there is more than enough evidence to indicate its usefulness in improving our cognition, memory, and focus. If you are just beginning, here are some quick tips to keep in mind.

Always find a quiet space to do your meditation practice, so that distractions are minimized. As you begin, your mind will likely wander and that will be distraction enough. You can set a timer for the amount of time you want to meditate. Similar to the Pomodoro Technique, start slow (about five minutes per session) and work up from there. You also don't have to meditate on the floor. You can do it in a chair, on your sofa, or even in bed. Just try not to fall asleep if you do so; meditation is about restful wakefulness. The key is you want to be comfortable as you're doing it. Remember to close your eyes and focus on your breath. Where do you feel your breath at its strongest? Let thoughts enter and depart your mind free from judgement. You don't have to reject thoughts or feel guilty if you have them; simply acknowledge them and let them go as you return your attention to your breath. If it helps, you can even think (or say out loud), "I am letting this thought go and returning to my practice." Do whatever you need to do to return your focus where it matters. This is key for training your brain. No matter what happens or comes up along your meditation journey, it's important not to judge yourself. All that matters is that you're dedicating yourself to this practice, and that is a good thing.

If meditating in silence or alone is too difficult for you, you can try one of the varieties of guided meditations. There are videos on Youtube, phone apps such as Headspace and Breathe, or a number of more in-depth guides you can search for at a local bookstore. Most research on meditation suggests that to get the most out of it, you should aim to meditate as consistently as you can at least four times a week. Don't worry, you can build to this consistency in your own practice, and you can take it slow. Even if you're only meditating for ten or fifteen minutes a day, your mind will thank you.

Some people will even opt to do walking meditations, especially if they're new to it. Like with other forms of meditation, the key here is to track your breath. For instance, every time you breathe in or out, you give the breath a number. Count to as high a number as you want, and take note of anything that distracts you or causes you to lose count. If you don't like the idea of counting your breath, you can also focus more on syncing your breath with your steps as you walk. Every time you inhale or exhale you also take a step. Then you can build to taking two steps per breath, then three, four, five, six, and so on until it feels too uncomfortable. The goal is for you to maintain focus on your practice, not to get to the highest number possible. You have to follow your instincts as you pay attention to what's happening in your body as you practice.

If you enjoy nature walks, you can also focus on syncing your breath to the sensory world around you in a way that prioritizes your connection to the natural world. The goal here is to focus intensely on your breath and body and how they interact with the world as you move through it. Begin with your feet and notice how each foot has contact with the ground. What does it feel like? What do you notice about this ground? Feel your weight engage with the air, your clothes, and so on. Feel the temperature outside, and notice any lingering sensations on your skin. You can zero in on different sounds, visuals, or smells in a similar manner. Again, the key is to focus on your breath while immersing yourself in your surroundings. In general, you'll find the world unbelievably peaceful when you take it as a physical reality around you without analyzing or judging it.

Once you grow some experience with your meditation practice, you can try using similar techniques of immersion and breathing principles while reading, eating, or even in social settings in conversation with others. It will help you be more involved with your life and more present, in the moment. Finding more of this presence is the primary function of meditation. Presence helps you concentrate, which helps you integrate more information into your memory. This process is intentional and purposeful. Meditation is a powerful tool for improving concentration and your overall cognitive abilities. Rather than waste your time on useless or negative thoughts and worries, you can focus on your physical being in the present moment. You'll be amazed at how much more you enjoy life when you do. As you begin your practice, don't overthink the process, and don't give in to analysis paralysis. Just focus on deepening your practice, and be patient with yourself. With regular sessions, you'll see notable improvements.

Chapter Summary

There is no secret to productivity - it's all about organizing your day in a way that works for you. Look at your calendar. Make a to-do list. Set reminders for yourself. Lastly - and most importantly - limit your use of technology. Training your brain is all about avoiding certain stimuli (including digital distractions) and prioritizing what will keep you on track. The Pomodoro Technique is your best friend in doing this, as are mindfulness practices such as meditation.

CONCLUSION

You have made it to the end of your reading journey, which may have felt like a lot to process at times. Don't worry. You don't have to remember everything, and you can always come back to revisit chapters as you put these lessons into motion.

While this book gives you a roadmap to accelerated learning, it's up to you to put in the work, study, practice, and get feedback. No matter what topic you're learning, begin by understanding these principles so you don't get stuck in the details. Learning those come later. Be sure to connect new knowledge with what you already know in order to help with memory, and use the Pomodoro Technique to train your brain and retain your focus. You can keep this handbook close by for whenever you want to re-read or remember techniques along the way to rapidly acquire your new skills.

Now think of a topic or skill you've been meaning to learn. Write it down and put it somewhere you will see it every day! It's time to get started. We tend to get in our own way by overthinking something or by not taking action. Remember: you hold yourself back more than anyone else in the world, which means, on the other hand, you alone have the power to hold yourself up and help yourself achieve and learn what you've always wanted to.

As human beings, we can grow and change and learn to an infinite degree, and it is this sentiment I want to leave you with. You have so much power and potential. Each day you spend not believing that statement is a day you are wasting. It may be the end of the book, but it's really only the beginning of your life-long learning adventure. All it takes is making that first step. Believe in yourself, and believe that you can achieve greatness - and you will!

YOUR FREE GIFT

Thank you again for purchasing this book. As an additional thank you, you will receive an e-book, as a gift, and completely free.

This includes a fun and interactive daily checklist and workbook to help boost your productivity through simple activities. Life can get so busy, and this bonus booklet gives you easy and efficient tips and prompts to help you get more done, every day.

You can get the bonus booklet as follows:

To access the secret download page, open a browser window on your computer or smartphone and enter: **bonus.john-r-torrance.com**

You will be automatically directed to the download page.

Please note that this bonus booklet may be only available for download for a limited time.

Resources

- Boser, U. (2017). What Do People Know About Excellent Teaching and Learning? Retrieved from https://www.americanprogress.org/issues/education-k-12/reports/2017/03/14/427984/people-know-excellent-teaching-learning/

- Groat, B. (2018, June 14). The 10 Principles of Rapid Skill Acquisition. Retrieved October 30, 2019, from https://medium.com/@BGroat/the-10-principles-of-rapid-skill-acquisition-3b8bcbb02092

- Vozza, S. (2017, May 19). Five Popular Myths About Learning That Are Completely Wrong. Retrieved October 30, 2019, from https://www.fastcompany.com/40420472/five-popular-myths-about-learning-that-are-completely-wrong

- Seven Guiding Principles of Accelerated Learning. (n.d.). Retrieved from http://thepeakperformancecenter.com/educational-learning/learning/theories/accelerated-learning/principles-of-accelerated-learning/

- Nguyen, T. (n.d.). 17 Steps To Acquiring A New Skill Faster Than You Thought Possible. Retrieved from https://www.lifehack.org/articles/productivity/17-steps-acquiring-new-skill-faster-than-you-thought-possible.html

- Meier, D. (2000). The Accelerated Learning Handbook: A Creative Guide to Designing and Delivering Faster, More Effective Training Programs. Retrieved from https://www.amazon.com/Accelerated-Learning-Handbook-Designing-Delivering-ebook/dp/B00EBAALJA/ref=sr_1_1?keywords=the+accelerated+handbook+dave&qid=1572331888&s=digital-text&sr=1-1

- Floersch, E. (2019, June 4). How to Develop New Talents: Rapid Skill... Retrieved October 30, 2019, from https://steak.life/rapid-skill-acquisition/

- Patel, D. (2018, November 21). 10 Proven Ways to Learn Faster. Retrieved October 30, 2019, from https://www.entrepreneur.com/article/323450

- Gkiokas, D. (2018, April 2). 80/20 Rule: The Concept That Will Change The Way You Learn. Retrieved October 30, 2019, from https://www.themetalearners.com/80-20-rule-the-concept-that-will-change-the-way-you-learn/

- Kaufman, J. (n.d.). The First 20 Hours – Josh Kaufman Review Summary – ConsciousED. Retrieved October 30, 2019, from https://conscioused.org/books/the-first-20-hours-josh-kaufman-review-summary

- Metivier, A. (2018, December 20). How to Study Fast: A Guide To High Volume Learning At Speed. Retrieved October 31,

2019, from https://www.magneticmemorymethod.com/how-to-study-fast/

- Anderson, S. (2016, December 1). 7 Essential Steps to Cram for a Test Without Losing Your Mind. Retrieved October 31, 2019, from https://www.studyright.net/blog/7-essential-steps-to-cramming-for-exams-without-losing-your-mind/